HOW TO
FLIP YOUR
BIZ
&
CASH OUT
BIG

ANTHONY CALIENDO
THE MAIN MAN

TIGER SHARK
MEDIA USA

How to Flip Your Biz & Cash Out. Big.
Copyright Text © 2020 Anthony Caliendo
All Rights Reserved
First Printing: June 2020

For more information on how to sell your business or buy a business please visit www.themainman.com or contact Anthony Caliendo at +1 561 265 1400 or via email to info@themainman.com

Front and Back Cover, and interior layout/design by: Tiger Shark, Inc.
Chief Copyeditor: Krystal Harvey
Chief Content Editor: Anthony Caliendo

Tiger Shark, Inc.
www.tigersharkmediausa.com

Paperback ISBN: 978-0-9962693-3-9
eBook and Kindle Version Available

PRINTED IN THE UNITED STATES OF AMERICA

TABLE OF CONTENTS

Anthony Caliendo
THE MAIN MAN

f FNBC Florida

in Anthony Caliendo

🌐 www.flipyourbiz.com

✉ info@flipyourbiz.com

REAL TALK ABOUT BIZ OWNERSHIP

If you're a business owner and you're reading this book, this might be your story. Let's see if I'm right...

You own the type of business that fuels the economy – a **Main Street** business: your dry cleaners, auto body and repair shops, hair and nail salons, restaurants, service businesses, laundry mats, small technology and software companies, print shops, convenience stores, landscapers, tax prep companies and franchises located on Main Street, USA. You generate max $5M in annual revenues and you pump every ounce of your own ingenuity and optimism into earning those revenues for your business every day.

Your business is your baby. It's like one of your kids. I have eight of them (kids, that is) so I can relate. You've had to nurture it, pay attention to it, feed it, clothe it, educate it, groom it, shape it, mold it, discipline it, reward it and you hope that you give enough of those things to it so that it can eventually sustain and survive on its own, right? And effectually, you want to be proud of it.

Fast forward. Your business is "all grown up." You've enjoyed varied levels of success and sustainability. Survived cyclical economic conditions: expansion, peaks and downturns. Navigated through the market like a champ and perhaps, had to adjust your marketing strategy ad nauseam in order to stay on top while the business landscape didn't care whether you did or didn't.

On the flip, your business may have survived incredibly well, with little to no marketing because, as a well-established staple of Main Street, your business has thrived on reputation alone for its quality or niche goods and services.

THE POINT IS, YOU SURVIVED.

Now, you may have been in business for 5 years or 25 years. And for several valid reasons which we will uncover in this book, you've decided that now is the right time to sell – to cash out – or start thinking about it. You think you have a good, sellable business, otherwise your common sense business sense would tell you to shut your doors and cut your losses, right? But the business has been good, it's provided income for you and your family and your employees (if you have them). You've seen growth. **AND EVEN IF** your business has declined and the writing is on the wall, and you're self-aware enough to know it, you're still convinced, "Damn, I've put all my resources and my lifeforce into this business! I know there's value in it and I'm ready to cash out BIG while I still can."

Not convinced yet?

Here's my **5 QUESTION CHALLENGE.** Ready?

1 Are you tired of all the stress?

2 Are you tired of all the risk?

3 Are you tired of all the competition?

4 Are you tired of all the employees?

5 Are you just tired of being tired?

Is this YOU? Is this your story? Then, it's time to **FLIP YOUR BIZ?**

98% of the businesses for sale in America are Main Street businesses just like yours. Truth and facts: 70-80% of these businesses will never, ever sell. What does this mean for you?

Well, this means that it's time to get into action. This book is going to give you the REAL TALK reasons why your business might currently be amongst that 70-80%. And if it is, **as your business broker**, I'm going to tell you the truth, not what you want to hear. But I'm also going to give you real world, practical, "do today" tools that are guaranteed to help you fix or change your business' circumstances so that you can get out of the trenches and get onto a smoother path to selling your business.

Why me? Because inside of three years as a business broker in the fickle South Florida market, I have been able to sell the impossible – businesses that many of my colleagues in this industry said would never sell. They said that sellable businesses must exhibit a certain set of circumstances; they fit into a BOX, which makes them sellable and valuable. Yes, it does make it **easier** to sell one that fits inside of that box but most business don't fit inside of that limited, tight and contained space, especially where I live. So, they're wrong. There are ways. And now that I've done it an inconceivable amount of times, I'm in a prime position to educate business owners on what and how we need to execute in order to properly stage the business before we list so that it's not an impossible deal. **We want to sell quickly and at the full ask.** That's what you deserve, right?

The good news is that now is the perfect time to go into prep mode, especially if you're reading this book during the uncertainty of the COVID-19 crisis. Economists and businesses alike were completely confident about the health of the economy in the beginning of the year, and, despite what you may think, all indicators point to growth this year, or at least rebounding because the economy is driven by our human behaviors. We're going to want to stimulate the economy more than ever after this wave of the pandemic. So, up-leveling in certain areas to make your biz more valuable is going to be more doable than you think.

Now, I know that some of the near-crisis, near death situations that I will talk about in this book don't apply to all businesses. There are a lot of strong businesses out there looking to sell that absolutely have run a pretty tight ship with really great operational practices throughout the years. You are the businesses that I build my model from when I discuss maximizing value and the variables that drive the value.

But, if you have work to do, then let's get to it! Let's roll up our sleeves so we can create the path to **FLIP YOUR BIZ and CASH OUT. BIG!**

Anthony Caliendo
The Main Man

CHAPTER ONE

THE SAD TRUTH

The pink elephant in the room is...do you ever know what your business is worth?

The sad truth is: your business may actually be **worthless**, and therefore unsellable. Before you jump to conclusions, the theoretical worthlessness of your business is not just about slow or declining revenues. A lot of businesses experience that and are still able to find good, optimistic buyers that see the value in acquiring a business and taking it to its next level of profitability as the new owners (especially if sales and marketing is their thing). Yes, one of the greatest indicators that the business is healthy and valuable is its confident revenue stream and cash flow. But it's not the end all-be all. There's a lot of other factors that will render your business worthless when and if combined with a decline in profits and cash flow.

It really could be a perfect storm that the weather guy didn't predict.

HERE'S A REAL-WORLD EXAMPLE.

Oxford Tech Enterprises, Inc. is an IT and software development company. They've been in business for 14 years and have 8 employees. They've operated from the same location for 10 years and the owner is a career entrepreneur and a chief strategist. The business is diversified; a sensible, strategic decision that he made 4 years ago so that he could generate income from multiple sources and from a multitude of services. However, 35% of the company's revenues comes from one main customer that they rely on to stay in business. Nevertheless, Oxford Tech generates $3.5M in annual revenues. The business is providing an income and a lifestyle for the owner and for his staff. They juggle, but they're paying their monthly/quarterly operating expenses to keep the doors open and the checkbook can prove it. Not bad. Plus, the owner has a really, really, swell and savvy accountant that helps him be "tactical" with the books, so they can be more "flexible" with how they show their take and their profits, and can carefully mitigate the business taxes each year. It's what every successful business does, right? It's the American Way.

Now, the owner is the absolute visionary at Oxford Tech; he should be the visionary. He really does have an exceptional internal GPS system and he's strategizing on a daily about how and where to allocate the resources and farm out new opportunities for growth. Not only is he the chief strategist, he's the chief executor too. He spends 100% of his time planning and 100% of his time executing. Sure, he has generally skilled support staff that execute the tasks, but no moves are made without his input on the precise steps to take to get the jobs done. He's also at the helm of lead gen and the business relies on him to open and close. He's a true hustler but it takes a crap ton of energy to be on it like that all the time - energy that the owner expends 24/7/365. But to keep the business thriving, it's necessary, or the business dies.

24/7/365 x 14 years and the owner is beginning to find it challenging to maintain that same enthusiasm and keep up his daily high-octane pace to keep the business, his staff and his customers energized and optimistic. There's been some attrition and also some necessary downsizing because similar businesses started cropping up everywhere and now, they have bright, beautiful online platforms where consumers can take full advantage of convenience and quick turnarounds. Initially, Oxford didn't seem to take a hit because they were well established and had a great reputation for personalized service. But after a few years of trying to keep up with trends, the company's revenues eventually begin to suffer. Time to be more creative with the books, right?

Suddenly, hustling and putting out fires doesn't sound sexy and dangerous, it sounds down right hazardous and the owner is tired of risking life and limb to revive the business every time there's a setback. He's pumped enough of his own blood into it and he thinks, no, he knows, he can flip Oxford, Inc. to fresh, new owners with an endless blood supply that will replenish the business and take it to the next level.

The owner battles with the idea of selling, though, because there's still some parts of him that thinks he should hold on for a little while longer. He incorporates some new marketing strategies and adds some new ancillary services hoping to stabilize and sustain.

But, after 14 years in business, it's time to sell. The writing is on the wall and the owner is done. He's ready to flip his biz and cash out big. He decides to immediately list his business for sale with a local business broker.

OK. WHAT COULD GO WRONG?

A lot. For starters:

#1: the owner had no foresight to plan an exit strategy while he was still sustaining his sales. He decided to sell after the business went into decline, after slumping sales, after downsizing, after the point of no return. These unfortunate factors are going to lessen the buyer pool right out of the gate.

#2: the accountant did his job, but did the business no justice. The last several years of business tax returns show little to no profits because they're buried in "creative," tax-mitigating accounting methods. A potential buyer is going to want a business owner to thoroughly explain what actually happened and be able to back it up. **Bullshit answers will get bullshit offers.**

#3: Oxford Tech is made up of a staff of generalists. The owner, unfortunately, has created a culture and an operation that is 100% reliant upon him in order to function efficiently. He would have to find a buyer that matches his level of skill, vision and daily hustle to keep the business alive.

#4: over 30% of the revenue stream comes from one customer. Lose that customer and the business takes a substantial hit. If that customer is not confident doing business with the company under new ownership, then the new owners would lose confident revenues at the start of the take-over.

#5: competition is mighty. Oxford Tech's new owners will need to restructure their consumer platform to keep up with its industry's ever-evolving business landscape. If he or she doesn't have the know-how to do that, they're going to have to put someone on staff or hire experts from jump to help them with this restructuring, which could be a major deterrent to a potential buyer.

The sad truth is: the owner of Oxford Tech has no idea how much his business is worth and that he has severely brought down the value because of long term operational deficiencies. He'll find a business broker and the truth will be revealed in his business valuation. He's blindsided now. He must either come to terms with the fact that his business might end up on the wrong side of the statistic or that he needs to take some time and restructure in a bad way to bring up the value and create a flip-able business.

REAL-TALK REASONS WHY YOUR BIZ WON'T SELL.

Oxford Tech Enterprises, Inc.'s story is so common. As I will discuss in the following chapters and in my Exit Strategy Planning, there are several factors that drive the value of a business and there are ways to maximize them before we list your business for sale.

I am also going tell you what buyers are looking for and **exactly** what drives their behaviors when deciding to venture into business ownership of an existing operation. For sneak peak, go check out my Serious Buyer's Checklist on my website www.flipyourbiz.com

But, getting back to Oxford. After years of watching scenarios like Oxford's play out in real time with so many businesses that I've consulted, I have concluded that, above all variables making a business not as valuable as the business owner thinks, there are 3 stand-out, blaring circumstances that will render a business virtually unsellable...unless swift, calculated measures are taken to neutralize further decline.

THE MAIN MAN'S TOP 3 REAL-TALK REASONS WHY YOUR BUSINESS WILL NOT SELL

1 **Timing:** Here is the way it goes with bad timing when making the decision to sell. I call it **The Inevitable Wrong**:

Most businesses will sell for the **wrong** reasons,

⬇

Because they are selling at the **wrong** time.

⬇

So, they have to sell to the **wrong** buyer,

⬇

And end up selling for the **wrong** price.

The Inevitable Wrong and the downward spiral it creates can be avoided if and only if the decision to sell is made at precisely the right time. To me, timing really is the chief factor that dictates the entire sales process and whether or not you can flip and cash out BIG, not small. A business owner has to have the foresight and the instincts to know when to start devising a rock-hard **exit strategy**; one that is designed to recuperate all of the time and resources he or she put into building a successful business. So, it has to be realistic and it has to be intuitive enough to account for what the remaining life cycle of the business will look like for the duration. The exit strategy is the end-game in the playbook. The playbook can't only contain the strategy to enter the game and dominate the game, it also has to have an end-game, the last strategic steps you take to win the game. When selling your business, the win is when you can sell at the right time under the right circumstances with the right conditions, for the right reasons, to the right buyer for the right price. Game Over.

2 **Financials & Tax Returns:** Here's the way it goes with the business tax returns. It's called "how much revenues can I make without showing the IRS all of the money?" Yup. I said it. It's time to get real. Knowing that the IRS can't police every business, American business owners and their accountants use every inch of the tax code to their advantage. Just like the owner of Oxford Tech, business owners and their accountants are "tacticians" with the books so that they can mitigate the businesses' tax liability each and every year. They do this by burying the profits. The problem with this is that, although the accountant is doing his job, he's not doing the business any justice: a dead giveaway that the owner has no exit strategy at all. The profits that the business is able to show over a sustainable period of time, during its lifecycle, is absolute key to the exit strategy and a successful sales process.

3 **Key management:** What does a day in the life of your business look like? Right now. Today. If you're thinking about selling your business, and you're not only the star of the show, but you're also the strategist, the executor, the opener, the closer, the fire-putter-outer, the engine, the oil, the fuel, the glue, the steak, the sizzle, the butter, the gravy, the fat, the cake, the frosting, the cherry on top and everything in between, no one is going to buy your business. Know why? Because you're not an asset that's being transferred to the new owners. Without you – the business ceases to exist. You've become **synonymous** with your business and therefore, it fails to have an identity without you. Hey – if you're all about legacy and that's it, then, so be it. Guess what, your exit strategy helps you define the vision and the future of your business. So, if you've come this far in the lifecycle of the business, you want to sell, yet the business is totally dependent upon you to stay alive: another dead giveaway that you have no exit strategy. A new business owner needs to feel assured that the business can sustain, grow and expand without you.

IN THE NEXT THREE CHAPTERS OF THIS
BOOK, I'm going to deep dive into my **Top 3** as
well as give you some real-talk advice on what we
will need to do to start assessing the business
conditions and tangible ideas to do some major
course correction. In the meantime, start thinking
about the real-talk answers to these 3 questions:

"DO I HAVE AN END GAME?"

"CAN I EVEN READ MY BUSINESS TAXES?"

"WHO'S RUNNING MY BUSINESS?"

SO, WHAT WILL A SUCCESSFUL SALE LOOK LIKE?

Let me end Chapter One with some optimism.
Again, I know that these near-crisis, near-death
situations that I will talk about in this book don't

apply to all businesses. However, if your business is suffering or is displaying value-deflating signs, it is **absolutely possible** to turn things around and create a valuable, sellable, flip-able business.

So, what will a successful sale look like? **First,** a successful sales transaction will have a "fire" business broker who will navigate the process from beginning to end. The beginning starts with planning and preparation, that's if you want to maximize the value of your business. If you're looking to apply band-aids and hightail it out of there, be prepared to accept whatever offers you can get. But if you have the time and patience to plan before you list, you're increasing your chances of creating a smooth path to a successful transition. You need a business broker, like me, who's as interested in helping you prepare as I am in collecting the commission check at the end of the sale. Again, I have sold businesses that were a difficult sell. I can do it. But it doesn't have to be difficult and nearly impossible if we make a few strokes of the pen and course correct.

Second, third, fourth and fifth: (2). a successful sale will have a good business with a good valuation that accurately reflects the value of the business.

(3). It will be listed and marketed by a remarkable business broker, like me, who's a **business match-maker** and knows exactly how to bring the right buyers to the yard.

(4). The buyer, with full disclosure, will be serious and smart, desiring a business that produces what we call "owner's benefit." The seller will be able to demonstrate t, with full disclosure, and be in a strategic position to expect a fair offer. The two will come to the table and negotiate a deal with the most agreeable pricing, terms and conditions.

(5). Buyer financing and due diligence will be complex and involved but I promise you, if the first steps in the process have been successful, there is a clearing in the path with a sign up ahead that reads **"This Way to the Closing Table."**

The Closing Table is a place of celebration and freedom. The seller is free to enjoy the fruits of his or her labor and the buyer is on his way to the freedom and enjoyment that he desires that comes with business ownership. And me? I take another W. I'm vindicated because I helped all of the players realize their dreams. It's a WIN-WIN-WIN for all of us and it's **absolutely possible!**

CHAPTER TWO

SO, YOU WANT OUT...

So, you're ready to sell. Why? Well, there are typical reasons why a business owner will say that he or she is selling their business: ready to retire, failing health, ready to explore other opportunities. They are all very legitimate reasons, especially in today's business landscape.

Truth is, the real-talk reasons start rising to the surface after some initial discussions and review of the financials. I truly believe that people who decide to go into business for themselves are courageous individuals that have all of the best intentions when they make that leap from traditional employment to business ownership. So, when conditions start to go south on them, they stick it out as long as they can and they feel like it's their obligation to continue to breathe life into the business, even during all signs of deterioration, every up and down in the business cycle and all twists in the plot. They get caught up in the daily grind and let acceptance set in. Honestly, it's admirable. It's commitment at its best. But it's detrimental.

Another thing: the ideals about business ownership and exit plan have changed; because the face of America has changed. Dare I say: the globe has changed. Look around you. Consumers consume differently therefore businesses operate differently. Products and services are introduced into the marketplace differently due to drastic changes in their respective industries. And the generation gap between our parents, us, our children and theirs seems wider than ever, especially when it comes to education, career, tech, work ethic and even entrepreneurialism.

No matter how cool we think we are, our children will totally remind us on a daily how un-cool we really are. And those of us who are business owners with Baby Boomer values, our kids are proud of that and they enjoy all of the luxuries, privileges and lifestyle that our successful businesses afford them. But guess what...they don't want take over the family business anymore! Millennial values and deals don't align with the Baby Boomer or Gen-X values. Millennials, God bless them, have an idealistic attitude about entrepreneurialism and they're totally fueled by it. I have a lot more that I could say about them but I'll save it for one of my other books.

So, herein lies the issue. Most business owners think that they have to keep grinding it out, taking the good with the bad, the ups with the downs, and continue to breathe life into a business with no pulse. They unfortunately decide to sell after the business has started to experience decline and, in some instances, decay. **And there is no exit strategy.** In some cases, the kids were the exit strategy so there's no talk of an exit strategy. The parents fail to map out the future of the business because they've been busy trying to build a legacy. Meanwhile, Joey Jr. is Gary Vee's biggest follower, has other ideas and aspirations and wants nothing to do with Mom and Dad's business.

So, as in the case of Oxford Tech, if there was an exit strategy, then the owner would have started staging the business for sale at the precise moment that he could no longer envision himself behind the wheel. Not having one could KILL the business' chances of creating the right conditions to maintain the value so he or she can **flip and cash out big.**

EXIT STRATEGY IS THE KEY TO FLIPPING YOUR BIZ AND CASHING OUT BIG!

FROM CRADLE TO GRAVE.

Boy, if I could spend at least 2 years with all main street business owners before they realistically see themselves exiting the business, I could really offer them some strategic ways to maneuver and position themselves for a more fluid, successful transition. Truly, the life of the business begins during its inception and its death is not when it "dies of natural causes" or becomes acquired, but when it becomes **unsellable** and dies for good. Having a plan or some semblance of one is the cure before becoming terminal.

So, the obvious next question is: "Anthony, when should I start planning my exit strategy?" Or in most cases, "when should I have planned it?" I know what most business strategists have said on the matter, but I'm going to give you real-talk, realistic ways of thinking about this.

First, let's chop up what the general phases of the business lifecycle are so you can understand what's happening and what you're most likely experiencing during each. I'm going to tell you when others say is the right time to plan your exit and then I'm going to tell you, a Main Street business owner, when the real-talk time to start planning is.

7 PHASES OF THE
BUSINESS LIFECYCLE

1 START-UP

2 GROWTH

3 SLOWDOWN

4 SUSTAINING

5 DECLINE

6 DECAY

7 FAILURE

Figure 1. The 7 Phases of the Business Lifecycle

❶ Start-up: inception. Oh yes! This is the seed. This is birthplace of the idea, shiny and new with optimism fueling a kick-ass USP. In **Cracking the Code to Success,** I say that this is when individuals put on their capes and gain extraordinary entrepreneurial courage – "driven and focused individuals that decide they have a story to tell and want to reap the rewards from sharing it with others. Building a brand plus achieving financial independence and security are key reasons to take that leap of faith to business ownership."[1]

❷ Growth: expansion. You're blowing up in a big way! Your shiny idea has more than gained traction and has become an income-producing product or service that consumers want and need. Your customer base is growing and cash flow allows you to increase your spend on things that will keep the business flourishing (marketing, employees, bigger and brighter product lines, multiple locations). You're excited during the growth phase. Why shouldn't you be?

3 Slowdown: peak. This is the small notch between growth and sustaining. It's an odd phase but a positive one; when growth slows down. This is when you're able to analyze all of your growth indicators, become totally aware and start **scaling** based on what you want to accomplish next.

4 Sustaining: maturity. You're established now. Congratulations. This is when customer retention and refining the operation comes into clear focus. At this stage in the game, you know you don't want to go backwards so you do what you have to do to try to prevent that from occurring. But maybe you want to start expanding again. Maybe you want to diversify. This is when these types of decisions should come into focus.

5 Decline: recession/contraction. You start going backwards and you have to scale down or downsize. That could mean laying off staff, cutting salaries and closing locations. It could also mean you have to skimp on quality (suppliers, cost of goods, competent staff) so you can decrease your costs of doing business. Like I've said my entire professional career, **"good things ain't cheap and cheap things ain't good."** So, naturally, there are more fires to put out now and you realize that fire-fighting isn't what you want to do for the rest of your life. This is when you know that if things don't pick up, it could be detrimental. Tough conversations need to be had.

6 Decay: depression. They also call this the trough. The staff and the budget have whittled down to what will keep the doors open and keep a paycheck in the hands of those that are dedicated enough to stick around. There's usually one last marketing push to drum up whatever business you can generate. The writing is on the wall during this phase and now, even tougher conversations need to be had with yourself, your family and your staff.

7 Failure: demise. Game over. Real talk. Enough said.

Again, your exit strategy is your end game. All that adrenalin and optimism you had during the start-up phase; the reasons why you entered the game in the first place, is the reinforcement for your end game. Your end game is how you will achieve the wins that you envision for the business as well as for yourself, personally, and for your family. No one envisions the end game being **business failure.** So again, timing is such a crucial factor when planning your end game; your exit strategy.

WHAT BUSINESS STRATEGISTS TELL YOU

So, my counterparts will tell you that you should/should have start planning your exit strategy during **Phase 4** – when you're sustaining. It makes perfect sense, because that is a natural choice point: it's when you start making decisions about whether to expand, streamline, diversify or just be comfortable with maintaining the status quo. Idyllically, they say, that one of those decisions during Phase 4 should also be whether to sell or not. This is when you should come to the table, bring in your reinforcements (spouse, key staff, business advisors, etc.) and start answering the following real-talk questions with crystal clear, sound mind and body:

1 Where do I realistically see the business in 5-10 years?

2 What will be my role be as the business changes and evolves? Can this business survive without me?

3 What is my business worth today and what am I doing to maximize the value in the future?

4 Is succession probable or even possible? If so, who is the likely successor (family, key staff, new buyer?)

5 If there is no probable, possible succession plan...then what?

6 Is there a life for me and my family after this business and what will it look like?

7 What do I want to do with the rest of my life?

It all sounds good, right? And pretty accurate. But...we're human. Suffice it to say, we get comfortable and we get caught up in the daily hustle. Sometimes we fear change and would rather roll with the devil we know instead of the one we don't know.

WHAT I TELL YOU
↓

This is what I say: start planning your exit strategy at the phase called **Point of No Return** AKA "I need to get the hell out and move on to the next big thing in my life. But before I go – I need to reap some rewards from the resources and sacrifices that I put into making this whole thing work. I want to flip it and cash out BIG!"

Phase **Point of No Return** is the **PRECISE moment you start having doubts**; doubts about your passion, your motivation, your faith in the longevity of the business, your faith in your products or services. It's when your inner voice starts speaking out loud and says: "there's no way in hell I see myself operating this business in the foreseeable future of my life." This is your point of no return. **And this point of no return can occur at any phase of the business lifecycle, right?** Think about it. If you're a serial entrepreneur addicted to the start-up like crack, then you might be ready to exit after Phase 3 and move onto another high! This is your gut; your internal GPS at work and no one can question it or tinker around with it. Just have the fortitude and the foresight to start planning the exit strategy with real talk answers to the six questions on page 32.

In other words, the point of no return is not necessarily when decline and decay have already set into the business. What we want to do is be able to recognize the point of no return before those phases. So, if we must put it in some kind of chronological order, call it Phase 4.5. Wherever it occurs for you in the lifecycle, it requires you to have ultra-keen awareness and instinct. It's tricky. This is what I will help you to do when we start strategizing and creating a flip-able, sellable business.

OH, THERE'S AN 8TH PHASE.

There's an 8th phase in the business lifecycle: it's called "recovery." Recovery can take shape in several ways. It's typically when, if economic factors affected the growth and sustenance of the business (i.e. like when the housing market crashed in 2008 – I know because this happened to me), then recovery is when the economy begins to turn around making it safe for businesses to re-enter those markets that were adversely affected; or even diversify and enter new markets so that they can stay afloat and rebuild. This could have been part of your business' lifecycle today. Again, I know because it happened to me.

If you are a business owner and you've been blessed; anointed with recovery, that means that you now have a second shot at life and now you need to do things a little differently than you did before. You're smarter, wiser and more strategic.

You're the Comeback Kid. You'll know the value of having an end-game this time around; an iron clad exit strategy, so you don't have to take lumps the way you did before. Plus, your staff and your family are counting on that.

Make sense?

EXIT STRATEGY = CASH OUT. BIG.

Simply: the exit strategy allows you to cash out, if that's what your end game is. But it will not only allow you to cash out - it will allow you to cash out BIG – especially if you prepare. The more time you put into preparation will only serve to maximize the value of your business and ensure a smooth path to transition. **You want to be valuable, not vulnerable** when you come to the negotiating table.

Later in the book, I will discuss in detail with you, key value drivers and everything that we need to consider before we list and things we can improve upon while the business is on the market.

Here's a quick list of value drivers:

1. Income and cash flow

2. Location

3. Existing customer base

4. Key staff/management

5. Industry/market sustainability

6. Assets

7. Competition

8. Ease of operation

The order of importance will depend on the buyer. But the main point that I want to drive home is that when we start positioning your business for sale, we'll be doing it with this essential question in the forefront of our minds:

"WHAT DO BUYERS WANT?"

After all, giving buyers what they want is the way to the cash. When I help stage your business for sale, I work all the angles as if **I AM** the buyer, not your business broker – and I'll get into that later in the book.

First of all, buyers (consumers in general, actually) want as much as they can get for as little as they can pay for it. The same applies here. And since it's one of the biggest, most critical investments in their lives, they'll be looking for the perfect business – one that provided benefit to you when you operated it and one that will provide him/her with future benefit after the transition. Again, we're going to get into the details about the buyers' checklist soon.

But, as much as buyers are looking for the perfect business, they're also going to be looking for ways to leverage themselves at the negotiating table. They'll be looking for weaknesses and holes in your game, and once identified, they'll add plausible strategies in their playbook to fix the holes after they takeover. Then they're going to use those holes as leverage to negotiate the selling price.

Meanwhile, as the seller, you will want to do whatever you have to, to negotiate the price as close to the ask as possible. So, what the exit strategy, and further, prepping the business for sale will do, is allow you to identify those weaknesses, make changes in the operation so that it can maintain or become more profitable, thus increase the value and cash out for a lot more money.

So, when thinking about "what do buyers want," the exit strategy will force you to analyze these things pronto:

❶ What do my books look like? (I will discuss this in the next chapter)

❷ Who is on my key management team and will they stay during and after the transition? (I will discuss this in Chapter 4)

❸ How efficient is my operation?

4 What are all of my exit options?

5 Where can I find a great business broker to help me navigate through this process?

Good news. **You found your business broker** so you can cross that one off the list!

CHAPTER THREE

NOW I HAVE TO EXHUME THE BODY

Relax, Pisan.

Yes, this book is full of cautionary tales and near-death sagas, as in the case of Oxford Tech Enterprises, Inc. My purpose in doing this is to urgently alert you and business owners like you to the everyday operational practices that might be killing your business.

Again, there are lots of business owners that are running their business by the book and they're absolutely prepared to load, lock and engage their exit strategy when they've hit their point of no return, whatever phase of the business lifecycle that it occurs for them. I acknowledge that, I recognize that and I appreciate that.

However, if you have some deficiencies in your operation, some holes in your game, I am here to help you identify what they are and to strategize on how to repair the damage. Being able to repair, restructure and recover are essential if we're going to flip and cash out big. It's possible and now is the absolute right time to do this. All indicators point to growth this year so, restructuring your biz to increase its "flip-ability" is absolutely possible. But you're going to have to trust the process. We have some digging to do. Grab a shovel.

So, in Chapter One I asked you to ask yourself this: **"can I even read my business taxes?"** What was your honest, gut reaction to that question? Well, you know that you and your accountant step into the war room every year. You know you both chop it all up and lay it all out on the table. You agree. You disagree. Trade shots, even. Someone might tap out. But in the end, you know that you both emerge alive, battle-worn, and one of you is waiving a white flag which just happens to be your business tax returns ready to mail to the three-letter organization. You're both alive. **But you just may have murdered the business and one of you is an accessory.** Which one all depends on the relationship you have with one another.

There's a battle of wits going on between you and your accountant. Love-hate. Because by and large, he or she is the professional and business owners rely on them for their knowledge, expertise, their ability to interpret the complicated code, and dare I say, their creative approach to the tax code. At the end of the day, their duty is to "properly" advise you just as much as it is to perform the mechanics of preparing the return. They're doing their job. And if you're like most of their main stream business clients, they know you're going to push it to the limit and do as much that is allowable to work that tax code in your favor. Which means in real-talk language: pay as little to the IRS as you can get away with. That's just the way it is, so we may as well lay it all out on the line and get comfortable with me saying it. **NO ENTERPRISE**, big or small, wants to pay it all out in taxes. They just don't. They do what they need to do in order to mitigate their tax liability each and every year and their accountants are the brains of the outfit, and they figure out how to get it done.

But here's my point: you did the taxes. You do the taxes every year and you report very important things about the performance of the business for that particular fiscal year and over a period of time. Your accomplice can read them but can **YOU** read them? Do you understand them? Do you know what they indicate about the health of the business? You do know that your tax returns are a snapshot of the entire business landscape, right It's not just something "you have to do" because it's the law. Think about it. It reports the profits, losses, your operational expenses (which reveals your operational practices), your staff and how they might live based on what you pay, your assets, your distributions and how you're living based on what you pay yourself, and so much more. Your tax returns should accurately report how successful you are and have been throughout the business lifecycle. So, you should totally care about what they indicate! If you can't read your taxes and understand the story they tell, then there's a chance that you really have no idea how "creative" book keeping and tax reporting may have lowered the value of your business. That's no good, especially if you're ready to sell. I hate to say it, but you may have become a business killer. And the manner of death? Buried alive.

A SLOW AND PAINFUL DEATH

Your business tax returns validate your business' financial performance. This is the first place that potential buyers are going to look to see documentable proof that your business is an income producing enterprise that pays you to own it. Let me restate that. **Potential buyers will want to know that your business produces income and that it pays you to own it.** Your business tax returns are supposed to act as documented, verifiable, believable proof of those two things. To quote a line from one of my favorite movies of all time, Jerry McGuire, they're going say this and say it loud, "show me the money!" In other words, they need to feel secure in knowing that your business produces cash flow. Here is what Cash Flow means:

CASH FLOW =

Income to sustain operating costs

⬇

Earnings to show profits

⬇

Owner's benefit that provides a lifestyle

⬇

SDE or Seller's Discretionary Earnings

In order to get to the negotiating table with a buyer, he or she must feel confident that your business produces cash flow now and feel very confident that they will be able to duplicate and exceed what you've done, especially if they improve the operation and make it more profitable.

SDE IS KEY TO DETERMINING THE VALUE OF YOUR BIZ AND TO CASHING OUT BIG!

Again, your businesses' tax returns over a 3-year period of time is the snapshot that will capture cash flow. If year after year, you're burying the net profit of the business inside, let's say, expenses, then you're essentially killing the value of the business by not being able to show and prove financial health of the business. Each year that you and the accountant avoid paying taxes, the value of your business is dying a slow and painful death – you're essentially eroding your shot at exiting the business, flipping it and cashing out big. Tough love: business owners can be penny foolish and instead of paying taxes, they do whatever they need to do to mitigate them, not realizing how this practice can ruin the true financial picture of the business.

EXHUMATION

So, now you want out. You're ready to liquidate, recuperate, regenerate and enjoy the fruits of your years of labor and sacrifice. The prospect of that sounds glorious, right? Because, in your mind, what you know you won't do is sell for less than the business is worth, right? Hell no. That's what you're not going to do.

So, what do you do? You start the process. That could mean that you employ an attorney or a business intermediary, like me, to get the ball rolling. You start to engage with them and you already have an idea of what you think your business is worth based on, perhaps, some rudimentary calculations and mental eval of the operation over the years. Now, a good business broker like me is going to get into the intricacies right away. I don't like to bullshit around and waste time. I understand from jump what you're trying to achieve and I know you want instant gratification. That's human nature. So, the least I can do is match your eagerness and get into the process with gusto.

The first thing I'm going to ask for is to see 3 years prior business tax returns, a YTD P&L, an asset list and a list of your inventory if you have it. **These documents are the Bible.** These documents are the bedrock to the question: how much is my business worth? If I can't look at your financials, then I can't complete a valuation. No valuation, no sale. I realize that the financials only tell part of the story, but it's the intro to the story and the main factor into completing and being able to explain the valuation.

So, I have your returns in front of me. Here's the line I'm going to focus on: Net Profits. Now, if you and your sidekick the accountant have been playing your numbers game each year to moderate your taxes, then you've most likely been burying your profits inside of your expenses or somewhere else. No judgement – I've already stated that no American business owner wants to give it all away to the IRS in taxes, so I get it. I have no dog in the fight! But, just stay with me on this. If you've been digging and burying and digging and burying for the last few years, know that you've been digging your business' grave and murdering it year after year. How deep is your grave right now? Are you 6' under yet? This is what I have to investigate.

Now we have to return to the scene of the crime, become grave diggers, me and you, **exhume the body** and perform an autopsy to collect evidence for the investigation like a C.S.I. This could get pretty complicated and dirty, depending on how deep is the grave and how big body is.

In other words, what I have to do is the complete opposite of what you and the accountant have done, which is reverse engineer the tax returns, and try to uncover and be able to explain the true story of the business profits.

There's a technical name for this process called: **Earnings Recast.** When the earnings of the business are buried inside of the expenses, both the expenses and the profits are obviously skewed and are not reflective of the true picture. When we recast, what we're doing is adjusting the financials by adding back to the net using a specific set of criteria (what can be added back and what can't).

So, during the investigation, you need to be willing and able to confess so I can help you revive the financials and explain to potential buyers what the financials may not reflect. The deeper the grave, the more digging, re-working and storytelling we have to do. And understand, recasting has its limitations. There will be circumstances where the grave is so deep that there's only so much that can be recovered.

At this point, this is when a business owner gets completely stunned that the value of the business has greatly suffered; due to a lack of understanding about how creative tax reporting practices have adversely affected the financial snapshot. Is this you, Pisan?

Don't believe me? Look at this:

$100,000 NET INCOME VS. $20,000 NET INCOME
$100,000 OWNER COMP VS. $40,000 OWNER COMP
_____
$200,000 (X) 3 = $600,000 VALUE OF COMPANY VS.
$60,000 (X) 3 = $120,000 VALUE OF COMPANY

Figure 2. Multiple of 3 Explanation

Digging the grave means that you're decreasing the value of the business by $3 for every dollar. If the net income showed more profit and officer compensation was higher then the value is higher by 3xs!

Still don't believe me? Let me introduce you to Roman Basi. Roman is the President of **The Center for Financial, Legal & Tax Planning, Inc.,** which is an insanely successful conglomerate of businesses that perform very high-level and complex consulting services for businesses nationwide. What's cool is that his company is **the family business** and he took over the wheel from Dad almost a decade ago. Alongside him, their law/accounting firm works on easily over 100 transactions per year, and in most years that total exceeds $100MM. And their real estate company has close to 300 units of a mix of single and multi-family residential, vacation properties and commercial space including retail, restaurant, medical, and commercia offices. He also tours the country with Dad performing lecture series and educates the public as a contributing writer in a bunch of industry publications. Did I mention he's also a private pilot on top of all that? And he managed to stay married to the same wonderful woman for 21 years, who puts up with his business schedule and his crazy. This guy is a freaking dynamo.

So, I brought Roman into a killer, complex multi-million-dollar deal that I was working which required his crazy knowledge and expertise in the game. With his involvement, we got the deal steered back on track and steam rolling towards the closing table. He really knows his shit.

Roman, break this all down for our readers about how essential tax planning and financials are for businesses looking to flip and cash out...

WHAT ROMAN SAYS

"Anthony is absolutely right in his analysis. I receive calls every day from business owners and brokers throughout the United States interested in our legal, accounting and tax services for their

deals.   No matter what industry, business size, entity type, or type of sale, my first request is always three years of business tax returns, the most recent personal tax return of the business owners, and YTD financials.   When I make this request, not only am I trying to understand the business's revenue, profit, basis, and liabilities, but I'm already analyzing the most advantageous deal structure based on your financial picture. When I say "most advantageous deal structure," I mean the form in which the business is sold.   Whether the form be an asset sale, stock sale, 338(h)10, or equity rollover, i am looking to build a strategy that provides tax minimization to the fullest extent allowed under IRS Code. A strategy that delivers the most net cash after taxes at closing.   That strategy begins with a request of complete and correct up to date financials.

Anthony is spot on when he states three years of business tax returns and YTD financials are the Bible. Not only are they vital to understand the business's   value,   selling   strategy,   and   tax *minimization, but for deal stability, nothing stalls a deal more than waiting on up-to-date or accurate financials from the seller. Whether it's the buyer, the lender, your broker or counsel for each party, everyone has an interest in viewing the up-to-date accurate financials. Also keep in mind the financials are going to be dissected, substantiated, and potentially questioned by the buyer. Depending on the complexity of the deal and the sophistication of the buyer, the review of your business's financials could be from the buyer itself, or an outside accounting firm like KPMG or Deloitte. From my experience, these accounting firms are going to ask for everything from general ledgers, consolidated financials by location, aging and payroll reports, inventory logs, etc., to support the explanations for the earnings recast. Explanations that must be accurate and proven in the eyes of the buyer."*

Exactly. So Roman, earlier in the chapter I told business owners that if they've been burying the true profits of the business over a sustained period of time, I have to now go in and reverse engineer the returns (exhume the body) so that we can get a true picture of the profits. Can you further explain why we put so much emphasis on the earnings recast?

"Well, as you stated, Anthony, the profit shown on a business tax return is generally not indicative of the business's true earnings. It's through the earnings recast that we capture true value by adding back non-reoccurring, unordinary, or one-time expenses that are not germane to operate the business. In adding back these expenses, profits and cash flow increase along with the value of the business. For example, maybe your owner's compensation and benefits exceed the market norm, or you have personal expenses on the Income Statement, maybe you have family members on payroll that are not necessary to operate the business. These are all expenses that need to be analyzed and added back to derive the true value of the business. Once the value is

understood and proven, we focus on recouping as much of that value as possible at closing."

Excellent explanation, Roman. When you and I worked on that major transaction in Key West, you brought your Senior Associate, Andrew Rohne into the deal and you both had this insane tool that provided an even more in-depth analysis to the sellers. It blew their socks off and I think it really solidified the deal.

"You're talking about our Tax Minimization Analysis tool! Well, in recent years, I have developed the Tax Minimization Analysis (TMA) which provides the net cash after taxes a seller will walk away with at closing. The TMA has become such a staple of our transactional work that I've dedicated my top guy Andrew to focus primarily on the analysis itself throughout our transactions. In building the TMA, I am pairing the business's financials to its entity classification (C-Corp, S-Corp, etc.) to not only determine the best sale structure as mentioned above, but also the

purchase price allocation. The purchase price allocation is the process of allocating the purchase price to the assets and liabilities of the business being acquired in the sale. It's single-handedly the most important tax aspect of the business sale. Just recently I served as counsel for a C Corp Insurance Company in California. The majority shareholder's decision to sell hinged on the net cash after tax he would walk away with at closing. My first request was three years of tax returns, most recent personal tax return, and YTD financials. Why? Because I needed to analyze how to best allocate the purchase price based on the Company's financials. Knowing I had to combat double taxation based on the C Corp entity classification, I had to first determine the personal goodwill of the seller shareholder. Personal goodwill is a mechanism used to avoid double taxation in a C-Corp asset sale. Defined through a number of Tax Court decisions, personal goodwill at its core is the intangible value that arises from the efforts or reputation of the business owner (seller shareholder). In finding such value through an on-site visit and business valuation, I was able to bypass double taxation by allocating 1.3 million dollars of the sale to personal goodwill. We ended up saving our client upwards of $370,000 in federal and state income taxes."

Damn, Roman. That's a huge figure. A lot of businesses have heard of personal goodwill but aren't really aware of how it factors in. And I like that you explained why purchase price allocation is such a major component of the sales transaction. But what happens if the sale structure disadvantages the purchase price allocation?

"Good question, Anthony. So, maybe you're a flow-through entity (S-Corp, Partnership, LLC, or Sole Proprietor) with an asset heavy balance sheet. But a stock sale is industry standard based on the business complexities of licensing, the need to assign complex contracts, or governing regulations. Last year I served as the seller's counsel for a transportation company selling for

16 million dollars. With 57 buses, 30 plus cargo vans, and a large warehouse, their balance sheet provided an asset heavy business model. Yet, the complexity of their industry due to multi-state licensing requirements and heavy government regulation, required a stock sale. However, in analyzing my client's financials I saw that their stock basis was 7 million dollars less than their asset basis. Essentially, based on a stock sale structure my client would have paid capital gains on an additional 7 million dollars, a net cost of more than 1.5 million dollars in taxes. Nonetheless, using my client's financials I was able to recognize the need to obtain a 338(h)10 sales structure and was able to implement the structure in the Letter of Intent stage of the deal. A 338(h)10 is a stock sale that allows for purchase price allocation purposes the tax treatment of an asset sale. We were able to bypass the licensing complexities and government red tape, while gaining the most advantageous tax treatment for

the client based on early recognition of the asset heavy model in the company's financials.

I hope this brief overview provides value and insight to readers. With twenty plus years of transactional experience I have seen financials in all forms. If yours are not current or if you believe there are inaccuracies, do not get discouraged. Understand you have resources like Anthony and myself to assist and walk you through the process to best position your business to sell. As the owner of a law firm, CPA firm and real estate company, I understand the lifelong work, dedication and efforts to maintaining your business.

Okay folks, do you believe me now?

RESURRECTION IS POSSIBLE

Roman and I can stand here in front of you and attest to the complexities of business ownership, not because we have insane knowledge in our industry, not because we're both Chi-town boys, not because we're both good talkers and good writers, not even because we're both good looking bastards in suits, but mainly because we're both successful business owners that have put on our Super Suits day in and day out for decades to build businesses for ourselves and our families. And now we're both in a position to pass our knowledge on to others so that they too can be successful.

We both know that it takes an incredible amount of time, commitment, dedication, optimism and just sheer determination to maintain a business and make it something you can be proud to say you own. In Roman's case, his father built a killer business which had a solid succession plan to keep the business in the family to continue its legacy. If succession isn't part of your exit strategy and you plan to sell, you **must** get your financials in order now.

What we just laid down to you seems terribly complex, and it is, but it's doable! If your financials are a hot mess, **resurrection is possible!** And even if your books are pretty clean, you could realistically increase your cash price when flipping your business by 30-50% if you spend 1-2 years restructuring and or improving on what you're currently doing prior to listing your biz for sale.

Right Roman?

"That's right, Anthony. Folks, it's mine and Anthony's job to ensure you recoup that dedication and effort in the form of dollars when selling!"

That's truth and facts.

CHAPTER FOUR

PHASE OUT TO CASH OUT

Let's talk about the owner of Oxford Tech Enterprises Inc. from my real-world example in the beginning of the book. That owner was the shit. He really was. He was the founder, the visionary, the chief strategist, the chief executor. He spent 100% of his time planning and strategizing and he spent the other 100% of his time doing. He was just as responsible for lead gen as he was being the deal closer. The buck started and stopped with him, no question. And he split himself multiple ways 24/7/365 to make sure that Oxford Tech ran like a well-oiled, well-fueled machine. The staff, all generalists, relied upon his daily input on all levels to get their jobs done. They executed "tasks" but they operated with little to no autonomy. I think I also described him (or her) as **the fire-putter-outer, the engine, the oil, the fuel, the glue, the steak, the sizzle, the butter, the gravy, the fat, the cake, the frosting, the cherry on top and everything in between.** Simply put, and outside of any economic or slow market conditions that could adversely affect the business, Oxford would have never survived without him because he was irreplaceable.

Now I know what you're thinking, "Anthony, what's wrong with that? Any enterprise would kill to have a genius, a true hustler, a "real one" like that to keep the business thriving and profitable." I say, "hell, there's absolutely nothing wrong with that..." **...unless you're looking to flip and cash out big.**

If you're looking to sell your business and YOU ARE the business, then it can't and won't sell unless you sell to an individual who is willing and verifiably able to match your level of skill, drive, expertise, talent and blood transfusion to keep the business alive and well into its next chapter. Becoming **synonymous** with your business and essentially, becoming the brand of the business is very cool if you're looking to establish legacy and keep the business within the family, which is something that should be well-defined and documented in your succession plans. And hopefully Jr., the Optimistic Millennial, joyfully takes the reigns one day.

However, becoming synonymous with the business is very problematic if you're looking to sell the business to new owners, who must be confident in their abilities to meet or exceed the business' success under their leadership. You are not a transferable asset in the transaction. If the business' profitability cannot be duplicated without you, then it dies. Remember, the buyer is buying the future of the business – the 30/70 Rule. Their decision to buy your business is 30% based on how you performed in the past and present and the other 70% is based on what they see themselves doing with it in the future. Yes, 70%. This is a huge freaking deal. If the future success of the business largely depends on you being at the helm, then you have to obviously come to terms with the fact that a new owner won't be able to operate the business and realistically expect to duplicate or triplicate your success. A new buyer is going to feel the same way. If they don't feel confident that the business can operate without you, then they will make a very cheap offer or won't make an offer at all. It's common sense, really. Let's dive into this deeper.

ANOTHER RULE

This is the rule of **Business Independence which states that a business cannot rely on or be dependent on more than 20% of "something" in order for it to be both successful and sellable at the same time.** Those "something" factors are: clients/customers, suppliers and employees. For example, if one client's business generates more than 20% of the total revenues or more than 20% of its costs of goods come from one supplier or vendor, and in this case, the owner's daily input makes up more than 20% of the businesses' functionality to operate, then the value of the business takes a sharp nosedive.

The key to establishing Business Independence is through diversification and diversifying your operation takes careful time, planning, intention and instinct. You have to know how to create the right mix of business conditions to keep it stable and on course for higher levels of success. That could mean diversifying your revenue streams, it could mean making sure that you have a healthy mix of suppliers and vendors in case one of them can't supply you your goods. And in this case, means stratifying the different levels of employment within the organization and designating what is called a Key Man, if you don't have one.

Think about it this way. **Having a sellable, flip-able business means having one that can survive without you** on all levels. Simply put: you're selling the business to new people and you're walking away from having any interest in the business. The interest of the business is transferring to brand new people who are buying it and want it to produce the same owner benefit for them as it did for you. It has to be able to satisfy this purpose without you. WITHOUT YOU. You get to go on to pursue other ventures or retire wealthy and enjoy the fruits of your labor. If you are synonymous with your business, then you will not flip the business and cash out big. You might cash out small or you won't cash out at all.

PHASE OUT

Let's evaluate. How many hours per week do you, the business owner, have to devote to the operation of the business? In other words, how much of your time, attention and resources is needed to make the business run smoothly and to accomplish the hourly, daily, weekly, monthly, semi-annual and annual objectives? Can the business operate without your direct daily involvement? If your answer is you work 40+ hours per week because the business can't function without your daily decision making, dealing with customers, prospecting, putting out fires, babysitting or otherwise, then you must start course correcting immediately, and phase yourself out.

This is difficult. I know this first-hand. Logically, you know that everyone in the company relies on you to make sure that the business sustains enough to give them job security, a paycheck and a future. Your family depends on you to bring home the bacon. Your customers rely on you to keep them serviced and confident in the business' ability to keep servicing them and provide customer satisfaction. And you know that no customers, equals no sales, equals no business. Admit it. You like being at the office or in the business environment. You feel a sense of accomplishment and fulfilment and maybe take advantage of a little escapism from other things when you're onsite. So, of course, you're going to be on the front line, in the middle and on the back end making sure that the ship is tight on a daily basis.

However, this is a huge value deflator. If you tell a potential buyer, and they will ask about it, that you have to put in 40+ hours to run the company (and the plus could mean 50 or even 60 hours), this is going to deter buyers. It not only deflates their confidence in the ability to keep the business running without you, it also weakens their vision of business ownership. **Buyers don't want to buy a job. They want to buy independence in the form of business ownership.**

So, if this is the climate and culture of your business and you're looking to get out, flip and cash out, you have to phase out. **Phase out to cash out, real talk.** This means you must find a way to lessen your involvement in the day to day grind. I'm not implying that you walk away and leave everyone to their own devices to run the business. You wouldn't do that anyway. You need to phase out in a strategic manner and do it little by little. It's going to take careful planning and more importantly, it's going to take time. You will need to create a phase-out plan, think of it as a personal exit strategy, and start executing before you list your business for sale.

DESIGNATE YOUR KEY MAN

The first step in phasing yourself out of the business involves gradually loosening the reigns and lessening the hours that you spend onsite. In this day and age of technology and the remote workforce, you can actually cheat it in the beginning by making yourself accessible remotely instead of making a live appearance every day. But before you can even do this, you first have to do a major thing: and that's learn to delegate. Before you can delegate, you have to designate a key man or form a capable, key management team that will take over your daily duties and responsibilities.

So. Who is your key man right now? Do you have someone in the organization that you consider to be your right-hand man (or woman)? Someone that knows the business innerworkings just as much as you do. Someone who knows and interacts with the customers. Someone you trust to work in the sole interest of the business and someone you can rely on to make decisions that benefit the business, the staff and the customers?

If you don't have one, then you need to establish a core person or core group of staff that establishes some form of hierarchy and organizational workforce within the business.

If you have a staff of generalists, then you're sort of in a pickle. If that's you, then you need to start making some hiring and re-engineering decisions very quickly, especially if you're looking to sell the business for the most cash you can get. This move might ruffle some feathers with the current staff. But you have to make these moves, and it has to be done without alerting the staff that you're doing it because you're selling. **It's going to be tough. But it can be done.** You have to lay the groundwork and crack the door open without giving it all away.

However, whether you have a specific key employee, a group of key employees or even just a staff of generalists, they all play such a huge role in the business – let's stop for a minute and recognize that. Think about why they're important and what do you do with them besides expect them to work and pay them for their time? They are the bedrock of the business' profitability and it's quantified and magnified by the effort and dedication that the entire team puts forth on a daily basis. So, whether you're planning to sell the business or not, you have to be in the mindset that they deserve to be taken care of and considered for the long term. This is absolutely truer if your exit strategy is flipping the biz and cashing out. You never want to be the guy to leave them high and dry, especially after they've put in the blood, sweat and tears to keep the business operating, just like you have. So, recognizing them and giving them some incentives to remain in the business shouldn't just be motivated by you hightailing it out of there and needing to satisfy a new buyer, it should absolutely be about giving them the security and future that they really do deserve as major players in the operation.

Now, if you do already have someone or a team of key management on staff that have some specialization and you're confident in their skills, now is the time to start having some discussions, making some agreements, delegating to them and reassigning or redefining their job descriptions. **Start phasing out.** Pay them more with their newly defined roles. Give them some incentive to take on more responsibilities because this is going to serve as a key and strategic move when they do become aware that you're 100% selling the business. And when that day comes, you need to be prepared to solidify some contracts before you list, and I will tell you why in the next sub-chapter.

Once established, you need to work the new workforce structure wholeheartedly, and allow them to operate with some autonomy so you're confident with phasing yourself out. Ideally, you should phase yourself down to about 20 hours per week, if you can. You're not completely out, obviously. But now the business isn't 1000% dependent upon your presence and input to function. **Make this your goal.** You can do this strategically and gradually over time so that it's not such a shocker to the staff, the customers and the operation. It's going to be a challenge to let go of certain things.

But remember, in doing this, you're not only redefining their role, you're also redefining yours. One thing that I discussed in the beginning when planning your exit strategy, one of the factors that you need to see clearly is envisioning your role within the company, especially after you've taken it to a certain level of success and phase within the business lifecycle. When you start phasing out of the day to day minutia, now you have more time to dedicate to the higher level, higher-focused parts of the operation. Now you can actually plan the next chapters of your life and what direction you want to go in personally after you flip your biz and cash out big. You might be surprised at what you discover about yourself as an individual outside of your business. Now, that may scare you but it's something that you need to uncover because after the business sells, you have the rest of your life to live with you.

ANOTHER REAL-TALK NO B.S. EXAMPLE

True story.

I recently sold a Medicare health agency. They (description of the business services) and had been in business for 7 years. I already had a good relationship with the sellers because their children went to school with mine. Now obviously, that's not necessarily the reason why the deal closed and it's not a prerequisite to having a successful closing, but there was a level of trust and comradery that existed, which truly made the waters smoother – especially when I tell you what happened.

This business has complex licensing and regulatory requirements that it needs to comply with in order to operate. Let me clarify. The licensing is not attached to the business, rather, there needs to be someone inside of the operation that holds the license in order for the business to be in compliance. So right there, this was a major condition that needed to be satisfied or no deal. No sale. The buyer that we found didn't have the kind of time nor the experience within the business to run out and get licensed. Obviously, he found the operation to be attractive and the business offered him the opportunity to meet his goals as a business owner, so the fact that he wasn't licensed didn't deter him from pursuing the purchase. However, without that licensed individual, there would be no purchase so he relied upon the seller to help meet this condition so that they both could score their win. An Offer to Purchase had already been made and agreed upon. The ball was already rolling fast and furiously.

So, the seller and I crafted our strategy and went into execution mode. Now, in hindsight, this is something that a solid exit strategy with solid key man commitments in place prior to the sale would have solved. And it's not that the seller didn't already know the strategy, but there's a difference between knowing the strategy and executing the strategy. Knowing is always half the battle.

Back to the story. The strategy was to have the key licensed staff member agree to stay on board after the sale. Critical discussions and negotiations were had between the seller and his key man. A very sweet, incentivized deal was struck and the key man was in and committed to a 1 to 3-year contract whereby he'd remain on-board after the transition and keep the business in compliance with licensing and regulatory. All was good in the 'hood, as they say. The sales process continued as planned with other contingencies and due diligence to address and satisfy.

This one was in the bag, though. Life was good. Everyone was happy. Or so we thought...

Two weeks later: Key Man walks into my seller's office and says, "Hey, just want you to know that I'm putting in my 2-week notice. I thought about it and I'm not comfortable with the deal." In other words, "take care, comb your hair and change your underwear." WTF?

The deal died that day.

A few days went by. I had to think of how I could breathe some oxygen into this deal. We'd come too far to just throw in the towel and leave it bloody in the middle of the ring. I had an idea, albeit a far-fetched one, but it was worth a shot. I called my seller.

"Okay. This is a long-shot, but do you have any former employees or any associates that we can reach out to that might just might, still be licensed and might, just might, be in a position to commit to this deal?"

Long pause.

"Actually, I do" he said. "It's a longshot but what do we have to lose?" Not a damn thing, because the deal was dead. We needed to try to revive it and we needed to do it by any means necessary. We called the seller's former employee who had left the business 5 years prior to pursue other opportunities. You'll never guess what happened.

As fate would have it, she'd just been let go from her position at another company a mere 48 hours before we called her. She had no idea where to turn and what she was going to do to survive or support her children. When my seller called her, she cried. She said that she's been praying all weekend that God would intervene and send her a miracle. Well, a miracle is what was that we contacted her and that she was available to fill the shoes of the other staff member that left us high and dry. She'd been an asset to the seller's company before she left and the perfect person to re-enter and stay through the transition and beyond. My seller offered an incentivized compensation package and a contract that was not only satisfying to her, but it satisfied the seller, it satisfied the buyer and it satisfied me. This was a gratifying FOUR-WAY WIN for all parties involved!

The deal was resurrected like Lazarus and we all eventually made it to the Closing Table.

We might have been bandaged and a bit bruised, but we made it.

WHAT NEW OWNERS WANT AND NEED

This is the moral of the story and the main reason why you must put a key person in place and phase out to cash out. It's because this is what buyers will want and what they will need. **And in the instance of the story I just told, it can and will oftentimes be a condition that must be satisfied or the business will never sell.** New buyers are not just buying the foundation of the business; they're also buying key staff and they need to feel solid that the key staff will remain a part of the operation after the transition. Will your key staff remain through the transition and after the new owners take over? Well, that all depends on the new structures you put in place as you begin to personally exit the business. **Not after. Before. So be smart.** Your goal is to create a highly competent management team or groom a highly competent individual who can perform in your absence.

And there's other things you can do to phase yourself out and streamline the business while you're getting key staff acclimated to their new roles such as (1). Ramp up your marketing strategy so that revenues continue to grow, (2). Automate as much as you can and invest in updated technology to make tasks easier and more efficient and (3). Start evaluating and documenting all of your internal procedures and processes. Do these things by any means necessary or your business is not going to sell.

CATCH 22

With that said, remember when I said that you need to find a way to incentivize the new key person or key staff when you start transferring higher level responsibilities to them? This is a strategic move. **Because by sweetening their deals early on, you're building mutually beneficial alliances and creating some assurances that they will be willing to stay on after the business sells.** You have to be proactive about this and you have to be able to relay the message properly beforehand without giving if all away WHILE trying to accomplish what you need to for the buyer. That's the Catch 22. Again, the new buyer is going to rely on this. There's some insecurity there: going into a new business without some degree of hand-holding in the beginning. They're going to want to know that the key staff is going to remain committed and that they have the same level of skill and know-how as you do (maybe even more than you), to run protocol and procedure. They need to see that the business operates like a hub that has a solid nucleus keeping it tight. This makes the business highly flip-able and highly sellable.

Your business is your baby. You've had to nurture it and give it all of the things that a parent needs to give it in order to sustain and eventually survive without you. Think of your key man or your key management as the caregivers when you're not onsite and well after you've made your permanent exit from their lives. Nothing will give you more satisfaction in knowing that you've put an iron-clad infrastructure in place that will ensure the business' success after the transition and into the future; and generation after generation of future new owners to come.

CHAPTER FIVE

THE VALUATION

Up to this point, we've discussed what I like to call the **"meat and potatoes"** of the sales transaction – some of the crucial factors that I believe can make or break the deal or cause a business to sell for much less cash than the owner wanted. Now this is my meat and potatoes based on my experience in this business, in a market that's notorious for "anything goes" style of operating a business. (Other brokers may have their own meat and potatoes based on their experiences within their respective markets). Again, this doesn't apply to all businesses that I've encountered. A lot of them have been cookie-cutter deals that fit nicely inside of the box of ideal circumstances with perfect operational practices. The transactions are smoother, but even cookie cutters aren't exact. They have their sticking points or nuances that we might not uncover until we get deep into the process.

A sales transaction, from start to finish, is an incredibly complex process, no matter how perfect or imperfect the operation is and has been through its lifecycle. This is why you need a business broker, like me, who, can not only determine how flip-able your business is, as-is, from the get go, but can and will also sniff out the obstacles, and put some corrective actions in place so that the business' value is maximized and positioned for a successful sales transaction. It takes time, trust, skill and instinct. But it can be done and I'm the guy who can do it.

With that being said, **my role as your business broker is to find ways to maximize the value of your business.** This means evaluating all of the side dishes that go with the meat and potatoes and making it a meal. In this chapter, all of the side dishes and all of the factors that go into determining and maximizing your business' value will go under the microscope. And the best way to do this is to show you the valuation process.

You're probably wondering, "what else is there, Anthony?" We already talked about shyster accountants, finding a good right-hand man – a "ride or die," even murder and exhuming bodies. Sounds more like a good gangster flick. I agree. I have a way of storytelling in all of my books that not only entertains, but educates my audience. I want you to walk away knowing more than what you knew when you started reading. I want you to get a good sense of who I am as a business leader and an expert on how to accomplish our mission – which is to flip your biz, cash out BIG and get to the finish line in the quickest, most pain-free way as possible.

So, in this chapter, not only will you get a glimpse into all of the components in determining what your business is worth, you will also get more of an understanding of what the buyer is looking for, which drives what types of offers you can expect based on their desires. It will also further demonstrate just how intricate this process really is. So, let's dive into it.

Key Measurables:

1 Financials: we've discussed the dire importance of financials in the sales transaction at nauseum. They are the intro to your business' story. Think of your financials as the frontline of communication. And in the case of flipping your biz, what they're communicating is how your business has performed over a sustained period of time. You must produce your last 3 years business tax returns and a current P&L statement in order to get the ball rolling with the valuation. No exceptions. We'll be zooming in on cash flow and SDE. Again, potential buyers will want to know that your business produces income and that it pays you to own it – demonstrating low risk in as many areas as possible.

❷ Age of the business: how long the business has been operating. Young businesses that are strong and successful can flip and cash out big too, however, the general rule of thumb is a good, solid and stable business is one that has been in operations for 3 plus years.

❸ Location & Lease: where the business is situated, for how long and the terms of the commercial lease. Location plays a major role especially if the business relies upon visibility and ease of accessibility to satisfy its customer base. The terms of the lease are equally as important, and whether you realize it or not, can be a real, stinkin' deal-killer if not negotiated properly.

❹ Employees & Key Management: who are the key staff that contribute to the daily operation, what are their roes, are they specialized in a key focus, and how much do they rely on the hands-on, daily involvement of the owner? Remember everything we just chopped up in Chapter 4.

5 Assets: these are the **tangibles** that are owned by the business including equipment, fixtures, inventory, fleets, properties and are extremely important to establishing the business' value, so they need to be accurately tallied up on your balance sheet. Trade Secrets & Intellectual property are examples of **intangible assets** that can be a little complicated to value, however, they are still equally as important to establishing the business value if your business has them.

6 Creditors/Debts/Liabilities: obligations that the business owes and must satisfy in the future. These are key to the value of the business and it must be stipulated whether or not they will transfer with the sale or be settled by the current owner prior to the sale.

7 Customers, Vendors & Contracts: a strong, confident and diversified customer base (new and repeat) not concentrated on one particular customer is key. The same logic applies to your vendors, suppliers and other contracts (i.e. cc-man agreements).

❽ Licenses & Permits: city, county, state or federal compliance in order to operate specific or specialized types of regulated businesses. In some instances, as in the case of my client, the individuals that operate the business are licensed, not the actual business. Recall what happened in Chapter 4? Be very mindful of this as you begin the sales process, because it's another stinkin' deal-killer if not handled properly.

❾ Marketing, the Industry & Competition: strong branding, differentiation and dominance within a particular industry creates the best environment and set of circumstances for new buyers to come in and hit the ground running. Having offerings that people need and want and being able to brand and market them to consumers is key.

❿ Scalability and the possibility for expansion/growth: a lot of optimism comes with new business ownership and knowing that the current operation can be built upon and/or expanded into new markets or even locations is essential.

Other important factors that could affect the sales transaction in general:

1 Pending Litigation: this is a hidden, potential liability that needs to be carefully examined before you even list your biz, whether they're **processing, pending, probable, possible or punch you in the face when you're not looking.** Regardless, it needs to be disclosed or else it could impact the entire deal.

2 Liens: creditors, including the 3-letter organization, can put a lien on your business for failure to pay your debts and obligations. Liens of any and all kinds can prevent you from selling your business until the liens are cleared.

3 Key Business Relationships: this is something to consider because if you have key, mutually beneficial relationships that pretty much hinge on the history, personal relationship and trust you've established between both of you that both businesses have come to rely upon, selling your business to new owners could impact those relationships. Weigh it out and have some discussions before you list.

❹ Current Products/Services in Development: if you're working on your next sure income generating product or service, especially if it's proprietary, keep working on it. It will enhance the business' offerings and boost sales in the short or long-term. More sales equals increased business value.

Value Boosters:

❶ Financial stability: the financials and supporting story demonstrate a stable, income producing business that generates great, sustained, confident cash flow and provides owner benefit.

❷ Business Independence – the 20% Rule: the business shouldn't be more than 20% reliant upon one employee (or the owner) to run the business, one customer to produce income or one vendor supply goods. All of these factors must be verifiably diversified and independence demonstrated.

❸ Customer satisfaction and retention: constant flow of new and repeat customers that produce new sales and residual income, and that can generate great referral business through reviews and word-of-mouth.

❹ Positive cash flow cycle – ideal AR/AP terms: the business must be able to demonstrate advantageous net receivables and payables. Simply put, the money is coming in the door faster than it's getting paid out.

❺ Niche market: the more unique your product, service and selling proposition is, the more sustainability the business enjoys, the more control it enjoys in its respective industry, and the growth potential really is limitless...as long as having a niche doesn't create an overdependence on limited markets.

6 Growth potential: buyers want to invest in business opportunities that can demonstrate great performance in the past and present. They want to be confident that under their ownership, they can yield the same and higher levels of profitability than their predecessor. They are investing in the future growth of the business.

As you can see, there are a lot of moving parts and lots of measurables when valuing your biz and preparing it for sale. It's like evidence. It could work for you and it could work against you.

Remember **My Cousin Vinny?** One of my favorite movies of all time. Now, if I'm your defense attorney, I'm going to be like Vinny Gambini. My job is to take all the evidence (factual and circumstantial) and present the best damn case ever to show why your business is a good business to buy and that the sales price is justified. Who do I need to convince? The jury. The jury is your potential buyer pool. They need to be thoroughly convinced and satisfied with our case so that they can put the best offer on the table to buy your business.

So, the very first thing you need to know before you decide to list your business is how much your business is worth. If you have no idea, then it's time to work with a business broker, like me, who's main goal is to perform valuation methods that will maximize the value of the business and be able to BACK IT UP with evidence. Don't try this at home, folks. You need a professional that knows what they're doing.

And you're in luck. Our firm will give you a **FREE business valuation** and save you **$2500** out of the gate. Go to www.flipyourbiz.com for details and how to get started TODAY.

CHAPTER SIX

I DO IT MY WAY

My personal anthem and the headlining song in my life's soundtrack: "I Did it My Way" by Ol' Blue Eyes.

One thing you will learn about me during this process of planning, preparation and packaging is that I always do things my way. That's what makes me unique and different from anyone that you will ever meet in life. My way means winning; never accepting defeat under any circumstances.

So, in the context of flipping your biz and cashing out big, my way always leads to **3 W's:** a win-win-win situation for you, for your buyer and for me. My way is the path to a successful transition where the wheels of fortune of the business lifecycle turns in all of our favor.

THE THREE-WAY WIN

- The Seller: You are finally at the end game and you're able to move on with other ventures, retire and finally enjoy all of the fruits of your labor.

- The Buyer: He or she enters the game of business ownership in a strong position and is set up to succeed to keep the business alive with endless growth opportunities.
- The Main Man: Me? I keep dominating the game and continue helping sellers and buyers achieve their goals and put them on the path to a smooth, seamless transition.

Pragmatically, and other than the fact that I'm a pro and a game changer in this business, there are several reasons why you really need to entrust this very complex and involved sales transaction with a business broker. Most business owners looking to sell automatically assume that they need to retain an attorney to facilitate this process. You can. But you will have to pay retainer fees upfront and worry about costly, itemized billable hours throughout what could be a very lengthy cycle. Plus, an attorney who is not specialized in helping main street business owners flip is not going to have all of the tools in his or her arsenal to value, list, market, match-make and navigate the entire process so that it is a smooth transition for both you and for your buyer. They lack experience and dare I say, they lack focus. That's a high cost to absorb before the bulk of the sales process even begins.

What a great business broker will do that an attorney will not do is this: (1). Take the time to know and understand your strategy and reasons for selling, (2). Take the time to plan, prepare and position the business for sale before it gets listed, (3). Package the deal and invest an enormous amount of resources into listing and marketing the business in sexy and engaging ways, (4). Target the right buyers and be a sexy match-maker, matching sexy businesses with sexy, savvy buyers, (5). Control price negotiations and go to contract, (6). Navigate through due-diligence, seller financing, documents and, (7). Get all parties to the Closing Table. That's an enormous investment on the part of the business broker, **who doesn't collect his or her commission until after a successful closing.** Understand, an attorney isn't going to do all that.

This is why a good business broker worth their salt, like me, isn't in the business of listing businesses. **We're in the business of selling businesses.** So, the only goal should always be to make sure that we do everything within our professional power and skill to help business owners create a marketable, sellable, flip-able business. Later in this chapter, I'm going to show you my way to a successful transaction.

WHAT DOES A SELLABLE BUSINESS LOOK LIKE?

Our goal is to position your business for success. We want to present a business that is as sellable and flip-able as it can be when we **first** list it. I will explain later why it's imperative to make this our goal out of the gate. When buyers search for a business to invest in, they're going to be looking for the right business. My goal is to make sure that we position and package your business so that it becomes the right business for a certain set of buyers within the buyer pool.

Sellable, flip-able businesses look like this:

1 Valuable: produces income with solid sales, good cash flow and can demonstrate owner's benefit or **SDE = sellers' discretionary earnings**

2 Provides goods and services that the market wants and needs and has an existing, loyal customer base that is easy to retain and expand

3 Established for at least 3 years with a desirable location, especially if good foot traffic and visibility is key to maintaining a steady and expandable customer base

4 Easy transition: the business changes hands in a seamless fashion so that there are no hiccups in the operation, no loss of incoming business or a mass exodus of the staff

5 Priced right and financeable: the seller and the buyer can come to the negotiating table and agree on the best price and terms to seal a deal. The business becomes even more flip-able when the seller is willing to extend seller financing.

Here's the thing, though, and keep this in the back of your mind. When buyers look for the "right" business, true, all of the things that I just mentioned are key. But, that's only 30% of it. Truth and facts: the 30/70 Rule is in effect, which means that when buyers make a decision to buy a business, 30% is based on what the seller did with it in the past. 70% is based on what they can do with it in the future. The value of the business is really all about the future performance of the business. The buyer needs to know that they're entering the game to win, not fold. He or she needs to feel confident that the business' lifecycle under their ownership and operation is going to produce the same and better success than ever before.

THIS IS HOW I DO IT

So again, when you have arrived at your point of no return, and you know that it's time to sell your business, the very first thing you need to do is find a good business broker, like me, who won't take shortcuts and whose main objective is to score that three-way win.

When I package your business for sale, this is how I do it: **essentially, I morph into your buyer, not your broker.** I'm going to look for all of the holes in your game, identify the inefficiencies and find solutions, and on the upside, recognize all of the things that you're doing correctly so that we can enhance them and make the business even more attractive. That's what I do. Because if I'm acting solely as your broker, I'm using tunnel vision and my goal is solely to get to the closing table so I can make my commission, without giving a you-know-what how bumpy the path might be. That's not a very smart approach because again, a good business broker is not in the business of "listing" businesses, he or she wants to sell and sell big. Listing doesn't mean a damn thing unless the business can be sold.

The thing is, most business owners really do believe that it's an easy process...until we get deep into the process and then they understand how complex and complicated it can be. It's not an exact science, it's more of an art form, really. Your buyer prospects are going to come with different expectations, different personalities, different goals, different wants and desires – they will each have their own checklists and a playbook of their own. This is why positioning the business and selling the business is an art – because there's different strokes for different folks and you have to know how to paint the perfect picture to appeal to your potential buyers. You, as the seller, need to be prepared for that, and my job is to prepare you for all of these variables we will encounter when I start my match-making magic.

So, if you trust my approach, once we get into the process, it will make complete sense to you. It's a common sense approach. What you will come to realize is that the serious buyer pool is very shallow so it's imperative to anticipate all of the issues that may present themselves at each stage of the process: from listing to showing to negotiation to due diligence to closing.

And on top of that, here's something else you have to keep in mind. No matter how shallow the buyer pool is, there's not even enough good, sellable, flip-able businesses to accommodate all of them! Is there an ass for every seat? No! And even a great business that's attractively priced in a good market could take 6 months to a year to sell. All the more imperative for us to really dig deep into your businesses operation and anticipate the roadblocks before we list, so that I thoroughly understand and can forecast how we're going to answer any and all concerns on their checklists. Remember what I told you and this applies to every aspect of the deal: **bullshit answers will get you bullshit offers.**

This is essentially the key to why I will play the role of the buyer as we're packaging your business. I'm going to identify the inefficiencies or inconsistencies, I'm going to ask you about them, I'm going to listen to your answers, I'm going to either accept them or I'm going to tell you right then and there what we need to course correct before it becomes a roadblock to the 3-Way Win.

So, yes, there are different strokes for different folks and that's especially true of individuals that are looking to enter into business ownership. But again, realize, the buyer pool is already very, very shallow. When we cast our line to find the right buyers for your business in the pool, we don't want to just drop our rods in the water and never know what we're going to catch, we want to be able to target the big fish and harpoon those bad boys. In other words, the biggest part of my job after we list is to be able to bring the right buyers to the yard. Before we can do any serious match-making, we need to do a lot of screening and vetting. This is another reason why I play the role of the buyer because I have to know how to be able to identify and hand-select the right buyers as quickly and efficiently as possible in what is a real intimidating task for some brokers. I need to be able to recognize their mindset and motivations from jump so that I'm not just casting the line, I'm precise and intentional when I present these buyers to you. I'm harpooning them and then pulling them up on deck.

THE TIRE KICKER

During this very involved vetting process, we're going to eventually face **The Tire Kicker**. We might face a few of them. The Tire Kickers AKA the "Wannapreneurs" are a dangerous breed of buyers who linger in the buyer pool for years, who, for some reason, enjoy being in the pool. They either enjoy **the idea** of being in the market to buy a business or they enjoy **the idea** of being an entrepreneur. They might have good intentions and each time they inquire about a business that they want to explore further some may do so with the good intent to buy. But at the crux of it, the issue with the Tire Kicker is that he or she is searching for the "perfect" business. So perfect, in fact, that it is impeccable to them with absolutely no flaws (as they perceive it). While no such business exists, they'll inquire, continue in the process, over-examine every inch of the business and keep identifying hole after hole in the deal. They have the "What If" disease. They'll keep kicking the tire. They'll flip the tire around and kick it some more. They'll kick the tire down the road. And they'll do this to business after business after business...but understand, the Tire Kicker will never pull the trigger. He's a "Wannapreneur," remember, and he's been in the market to buy a business for years. Know why? He or she has a real problem with risk. They're terrified of risk. And for that reason, and that reason alone, they will never get in the game. We need to quickly identify this breed so that we can keep focused and stay in the game. Meanwhile – game over for them.

THE SERIOUS BUYER

Here's our guy. The Serious Buyer. The Serious Buyer is as motivated to buy as you are to sell. When I play the role of the buyer when we're preparing your business for sale, I'm playing this guy's role.

The Serious Buyer will start by asking vital, common sense questions:

⬇

How much can I make in this business?

How much is the seller making now?

Can I make more in this business than the seller is making now?

How easy or difficult is it to operate this business?

If this is such a good business, then why is it for sale?

Right? Common sense. These are the surface questions that they will be seeking the answers to about every business they inquire about right from the start. It's the introduction of the story. If they get attractive answers to those surface questions, then they're ready to hear the rest of the story.

There's a lot of factors that will drive your buyers' decisions-making on what is the "right" business for them. I want to lead them to the right business (I want your business to be the right business), but I have to know what makes them tick, what motivates them to buy, what would deter them and what would be deal-breakers. That's all a part of match-making. I'm not going to fix them up on a blind date with a brunette when I know they only date blondes. However, I might find them a dirty blonde and present it as option for them to consider. Because the basics that dictate their decision to buy your business on a gut level are really basic: they need options, they need as much information as possible and they need to know that they will be protected in whichever business they decide to seriously pursue. And on a primal level – they need to know that the business is going to provide a living and a lifestyle for them that they feel they can't achieve as an employee in the traditional workforce.

So, the Serious Buyer will come with his game face on. He comes to play and he wants to win. We want him to win because that's an automatic win for us, right? He will have his playbook with him; I call it The Serious Buyer's Checklist. For quick reference, I put the checklist in Appendix C of the book and you can also find it on my website at www.flipyourbiz.com. That's just how important this checklist is. I put it in three places. That's because it's going to help us zero in on the essentials of what buyers are looking for so that we can position and package your business to meet their criteria as closely as possible. These are the set of circumstances that will either persuade them to buy or run away from the deal. And remember the 30/70 Rule. 30% of his criteria will most likely be based on what you've done with the business in the past and the present. 70% will be based on what he or she can do with it in the future.

So, after we list your business, I am now on the front line of communication for all buyers and their agents when they inquire about the listing. I have to make a great impression on them just as much as I need to do my due diligence and employ my vetting process on them. I'm going to be able to determine if he or she is a serious player (vs. a Tire Kicker) because they will have their checklist and they're going to be making mental checks on it as we go through the entire process of determining if we're all a good fit. Here it is:

THE SERIOUS BUYERS' CHECKLIST:

☑ Is the business broker legitimate and is he willing to take time with me?

☑ Are there options for me to explore?

☑ Is the business I'm inquiring about viable and legitimate for me to explore?

☑ Why is the business I'm inquiring about for sale? What's wrong with it?

☑ Is the seller willing to take the time to meet with me, be transparent and show me the business operation?

☑ How much can I make in this business and will I make what I need to provide me with the lifestyle I want?

☑ How much is the business making now? Can they show me the money?

☑ Is the business earning enough income to sustain the operating costs and provide cash flow? Can I realistically sustain that and even build on it?

☑ Is the business in a secure market or industry?

☑ Can I expand it? Are there growth opportunities?

☑ How easy is the business to operate?

☑ Will key staff stick around after I take over?

☑ Do I like the business? Do I like the location? Will it help me reach my personal goals?

☑ Can I see myself dedicating the majority of my time to making this business successful?

☑ Is the price negotiable?

☑ Can I use inefficiencies in the operation as leverage at the negotiating table? Can I correct the inefficiencies?

☑ Is the business financeable and will the seller extend seller financing?

☑ How invested is the seller and the broker into making sure I succeed in the business? Will they be available to me after the closing?

☑ How smooth will the transition be? Will I lose customers or staff?

☑ Can I flip the business in the future?

And there will be more questions on the checklist as we get deeper and deeper into the process. Our answers to these questions are imperative to closing the deal. At the risk of sounding repetitive: bullshit answers get bullshit offers – or no offers.

CATFISH DEALS.

So, this is what it all boils down to. If there is one take-away from this chapter, then let this be it. This is what I was talking about when I said that we need to address all issues out of the gate and before we list. Don't become what I call a "Catfish Deal." This is what we are trying to avoid. We avoid this by playing the role of the serious buyer; isolating and identifying the roadblocks early. We avoid this by course correcting and implementing corrective actions that can either be completed before we list or that will build momentum and produce results while we are in ensuing phases of the process. We avoid this by properly valuing the business and listing it for the right price out of the gate. We avoid this by not selling promises because the serious buyers, the ones we want, will not engage us if they think we're full of shit.

So, this is what a catfish deal is. A catfish deal is a listed business, which becomes a bottom feeder, that winds up at the bottom of the lake. This is a business that becomes difficult to sell; unsellable un-flip-able. It becomes a stale listing. THIS is a business that fails to prepare before it is listed for sale. It looks good and shiny on the outside but it's all messed up on the inside. It's a catfish deal. A real poser.

Now, I do understand that there will be certain circumstances where a business owner is looking to sell as quickly as possible. A lengthy preparation process isn't feasible. And in those instances, I do have an iron-clad (not guaranteed) roadmap for these businesses, provided that the business isn't an impossible deal to begin with. If it is, the higher the probability of it becoming a Catfish deal.

The longer the business is listed and the more we make modifications to the listing (changing the details or lowering the price) trying to make it more appealing to the smart buyers, the more we ruin its chances of ever getting any inquiries, even from the Tire Kickers.

MY 12-STEP PATH TO A SMOOTH TRANSITION

Here is my step-by-step roadmap of what you can expect on my path to successfully flipping your biz and cashing out **BIG:**

1. The Main Man Evaluation

This is my initial meeting with you, the business owner. We make our first impressions upon one another: me as your trusted business broker and you as an eager business owner with a sellable business. I'll ask you ½ dozen questions and determine **if your business is actually sellable** in its current state or if we need to stop, course-correct and devise an exit strategy prior to selling the biz.

2. Review the Financials

I analyze your last 3 years business tax returns and a current P&L statement to see how your business is structured and what the financial landscape is. I need to get a sense if your business is going to be difficult to sell or if it's a cookie-cutter, by-the-book business. **Trust is established between us** and if we can't establish trust during this step, then the path to a smooth transition becomes bumpy from the start. Don't become an impossible deal.

3. Valuation & Pricing

We do things my way. I value your business based on all of the value driving factors we discussed in Chapter 5. I decide where to go to market with your business based on my expertise and precision-focused method of pricing.

4. Listing & Marketing

We create sexy, enticing marketing material and decide where to list the business for sale (I have access to the top global business listing platforms) and we do this in a confidential manner. **Confidentiality is key** because most business owners do not want to divulge to staff, current clients and vendors that they are selling the business. So, the marketing needs to highlight the most fantastic and stand-out facts about the business without giving away its identity.

5. Buyer Screening & Match-making

I'm the "match.com" of the business brokers. Here's the thing: once we list your business, buyers will appear instantly and plentifully. My staff and I have to be able to **vet buyers and weed out the serious ones from the tire kickers** out of the gate. We don't have time to waste and we have a sure-fire, fail-proof system in place that helps us build a database of viable candidates that are ready to pull the trigger.

6. Buyer & Seller First Date

At this point in the transaction, based on my screening and match-making skills, I will set you and your potential buyer up on your first date. I'm the chaperone. I explain to each of you what my role will be for duration of the process. I have to be as committed to the buyer and his or her desires as I am to yours, as the seller. So, in essence, I represent the "transaction." **I am a transactional broker** and this is how I maintain balance between all of the players from you, to the buyer, to the accountants and attorneys, the bank, the underwriters, the landlords, and everyone that will play a distinct and important role in this complex process. In any event, during the first date, I know you might not fall in love at first sight but my innate instincts will let me know right away if there's going to be a second date. My gut, call it a sixth sense, is usually "dead-on-balls" accurate.

7. Offer to Purchase

At this stage of the game, the buyer has reviewed the financials, the operation and can envision themselves owning and operating the business long-term. The buyer extends his Offer to

Purchase (Letter of Intent) with contingencies for your acceptance.

8. First Round: Financial Due Diligence

An in-depth review of the financials is performed and the conditions must be cleared. Based on what is discovered, the original Offer to Purchase is either accepted or re-submitted.

9. Second Round: Internal Ops Due Diligence

This is when the company's internal operation is put under the microscope. The buyer will examine the operational procedures, marketing, the employees and their salaries, contracts and benefits, the customers, vendors, suppliers are examined, as well as inventory, leases, vehicles and all of the nuts and bolts in how the business runs and sustains itself. The buyer must be satisfied that he or she can maintain the operation and that there is room for growth and bigger profitability.

10. Asset Purchase Agreement (APA)

Believe it or rot, THIS is the stage of the game when shit becomes real because this is when the buyer commits. Any deposits go hard and the buyer has committed to the deal. He is all in like Texas Hold 'Em. Any conditions or contingencies not met in the Offer to Purchas such as buyer financing (SBA. seller financing, bank), leases, etc. will roll into the APA. Alert: this is where death of the deal can occur because this is when deposits become non-refundable and the deal is supposed solidify. WITHCUT this, there's no commitment. There are 3 factors that can occur during this phase that could make the deal go South:

- Time: too much time transpires. It's a deal killer
- Attorneys and in some cases, accountants: they can kill the deal with non-sensical input
- Landlords and leases: in some cases, the landlords will get the "eff-its" and not do what is in the best interest of the sale or

comply with SBA financing to change the terms of the lease

If we can get past the APA, we are climaxing now. This is when we race to the finish line.

11. Final Stages of Closing

The best way to describe this phase is like this: this is like when you're moving and you've cleared away all of the big things and realize how much small shit in boxes you have left to move. Any and all outstanding conditions and documentation is satisfied during this phase to include leases, key-man and employee contracts, seller notes, etc. Once we finalize these details, we breathe.

12. The Closing Table

You have a closing date and all of the players in the game get to realize and relish in all of the hard work and diligence it took to get to the closing table. This is when the Three-Way Win becomes realized: the buyer realizes business ownership, the seller realizes freedom and me, I realize that the Main Man has done it again and I can write the next chapter in my success story.

And how long will the 12 Step Path take? Realistically, it will take anywhere from 9 months to sometimes, 2 years to get to the closing table. It depends on the level of difficulty and it depends upon all of the nuances you may face, which happen to even the most cookie-cutter deals. A business with tax returns so clean you could eat off of them could face delays in selling because, for example, specialized licensing that an individual must obtain (vs. the business) in order to own and operate. You see, the process is incredibly complex and no two deals are alike. My job is to make a marriage made in heaven so that all parties are satisfied in the end.

This is **My Way**. Remember, I have to control the process because believe me, this type of transaction will take us all on an emotional rollercoaster ride. I need to be the guy controlling the ride so that we all maintain our sanity and our faculties during the process. When I package your business to become flip-able, I structure it as if I'm the buyer and I hope my approach makes as much sense to you as it does to me. This is all a part of me establishing your trust and establishing upfront that I'm not just in it, I'm in it to win it. I'm not in the business of just listing businesses. As a business broker, I have my own personal goals that need to be met in this game, and it's not to list and lose – it's to achieve that 3-Way Win for you, the buyer and for myself.

CHAPTER SEVEN
NEXT STEPS TO FLIP YOUR BIZ

"So, what's my next move, Anthony?" That's what you should be asking yourself right now.

The goal of this book is to give business owners looking to flip their biz **an arsenal of introductory information** that will not only give you some insight about what you should know, how you should prepare, roadblocks you could face, but to also give you the motivation to **take action**. If you want to flip your biz and cash out BIG, you need to take action. As I would put it in "my way," you have to grab your ccjones and take the leap from "just thinking about t" to "doing it." That goes for the Boss Ladies too. There's no better time than the present to start putting that exit strategy into motion. If you have no exit strategy, but know you need or want to exit, you have to put the wheels into motion and get prepared. Now.

The point I wanted to get across in this book, and I hope that I have, is that the path from "just thinking about it" to the Closing Table will be a long one, with a crap ton of twists and turns – some anticipated and others, not so much. One of my very good associates in this business once said to me, "a sales transaction will die at least 3 times before the deal is done." That's the truest statement ever said. But, it's not how many times the deal dies, it's about having someone on the team that has the instinct and the expertise to put the deal on life-support and then pump new blood into it so it can survive. But from the very start, there's strategy involved. There's packaging and re-packaging involved. There's storytelling involved. There's ingenuity involved. There are essential skillsets necessary to get from point A to B, from B to C, from C to D and so-on. You need a damn good business broker at the helm that has all of those skills and more, and who's not afraid to grab his own cajones to get the deal done. If I'm telling you to grab yours, then you better believe I'm grabbing mine so that we can get to the Closing Table as smoothly as we possibly can...And it all starts with one essential component: TRUST. You putting your trust in me to get the job done and me putting my trust in YOU that you'll trust ME to get the job done. In other words, "you helping me help you."

The key to you trusting me means me not telling you what you want to hear, rather, me telling you the truth. This is a mantra that I've used for decades in all of my various businesses. If you ever had a chance to hear my ads, then you'll know that's the truth. What it really means is putting the client's best interests above my own, even if I lose the deal because some can't really handle the truth and they walk away. Me telling you what you want to hear means that I only care about lining my pockets, not yours. In this deal, there are three major players' livelihoods at stake: yours, your buyer's and mine. We can't afford to play around with the truth. Being a transactional broker means that I have to establish this trust and truth with all parties involved, or no deal. First and foremost, knowing the truth about the status of your business is essential in getting this job done. I need to know every detail in order to execute and do what I do best, and that's get to the Closing Table. And with stats showing that 70-80% of businesses that list never sell, the odds are already stacked. Our goal is to be in that 20-30% of businesses that successfully sell and transfer to new buyers that keep the business alive and thriving. We can do it. But you have to trust me.

Before we can even list your business, I need to know three key things:

❶ What is the true, current status of your business?

❷ What are you doing right and what could you be doing wrong?

❸ What do you need to do to fix what's wrong? Once I know those three key things, then I launch the action sequence – create the story. It takes a chief strategist and storyteller to be able to package a business to become fit to flip and cash out big.

As a lifelong salesman, business owner and entrepreneur, I've written and sold stories all of my life – all successful entrepreneurs have, including you. In fact, in **Cracking the Code to Success**, I say, "entrepreneurship starts with driven and focused individuals that decide they have a story to tell and want to reap the rewards from sharing it with others." And that's what it's all about, no matter what line of business you decide to go in, no matter what your vision is. For me, sales is in my DNA, so I always knew that no matter what business venture I pursued, my sales prowess would always keep me relevant and keep my businesses strong and thriving.

Just like the owner of Oxford Tech Enterprises, Inc. at the beginning of this book, I am the visionary in all of my companies. Notice I said companies, plural. Having this valuable, 30+ years of experience of business ownership gives me such a unique perspective and keen senses as a business broker, because I've seen it and done it all as a business owner. I've had the tug-of-wars with accountants. I've endured endless employee turnover. I've created marketing genius only to have the market crash. I've had successes and I've had failures. I've had to reinvent myself and recover from failures a bunch of times. I don't need to tell you that it takes vision, it takes strategy, it takes storytelling and it takes a whole lot of guts. Believe me, I've walked in your shoes for one million miles and back. So, I got your back.

My point is, in order for me to tell your story, I need to know your story. Once I know your story, I can bring it to life and paint the picture like Picasso so we can sell your business for the highest cash price as possible.

A TRUE STORY

I'm a cigar connoisseur. There's nothing like enjoying a stick on my patio with Ol' Blue Eyes and a glass of vino. By the way, I'm never unwinding. I'm always plotting my next moves.

Well, on one such occasion, I had the Father-in-Law on the porch with me, who loves cigars just as much as I do. "Pop," I said in between long, satisfying drags. "Let's open up a cigar bar, what do you say?"

"Sure, Ant," he replied, taking a long pull from his stick. A few months later, we had our very own cigar lounge. And what a place it was – the ultimate Man Cave. We had purchased it from a trademark attorney, who'd also loved cigars and had decided to take a gamble in the cigar biz. His gamble ended a couple years later and Pop and I took over with all the gusto and enthusiasm any new business owner could have. It was supposed to be our little "cash" business that we could have and hold for the rest of our lives. Something to make our hobby more enjoyable, really. A place to take meetings. A place to socialize with other cigar enthusiasts. It was already profitable (so the books claimed) so all we really had to do was sit back and enjoy our new toy.

But we had big dreams, Pop and I. We had a vision and a hot story to tell. We remodeled. We shredded through all kinds of red tape and yellow tape to get it licensed as a restaurant and beer & wine establishment in an area of the city that had never done it before. We marketed it like nobody's business. We had weekly and monthly events that would bring guys and big spenders to the cave – car shows, bike nights, poker nights. We served man cave food. We did shows. We made so many improvements that anything we earned on top of what the previous owner was generating was supposed to be gravy. Right?

Wrong. Make a long story short, we decided to hang it up after two years of the hardest work and effort of our lives. Suffice it to say, we decided to sell our cigar lounge when we came to terms with the fact that it just wasn't producing results that we hoped for. We wanted to flip it, cash out (big or small), and move on to the next venture. So, we hired a business broker to make it easier on ourselves and the process was a shit show. Now, here I am doing the right thing and putting this transaction into the hands of a professional so that I can increase my odds of selling and walking away satisfied. That was the smart thing to do. They locked me into a year long listing agreement and did no work at all. No marketing. No buyer screening. No match-making. And that's largely due to the fact that they put no effort into helping me prepare and stage the business for sale before listing it in the first place. Knowing what I know now, there were several operational and financial areas where Pop and I could have improved so that we could maximize the value of the shop and increase our chances to cash out bigger.

Without going into all the gory details, in the back of my mind I know that enduring that whole experience is what inspired me to pursue business brokering in the first place. Because my first mistake when Pop and I decided to buy a cigar business was that we failed to hire a business broker. We literally acquired a business based on a hand-shake and ended up getting burned in the end. A razor sharp business broker would have steered the deal in the right direction for us, sniffed out a prime location, and performed all of the due-diligence on an existing cigar business for us so that all of us could have scored a win: the seller, Pop and I and the business broker. Now, we did hire a business broker when we decided to flip the business but it was the most unorganized and uneventful process on planet Earth. He wasn't razor sharp at all. He didn't engage and control the process at all. So, my second mistake was that I just didn't get the right business broker to represent the transaction instead of his pocket.

And so, without having any experience at all with business brokering at the time, my instincts and experience as a kick-ass business person said, "Anthony, you've been brokering all your life. You've been a deal-maker all your life. You can do this and do it better than any other business broker in the game." You know that statistic I keep repeating to you that 70-80% of businesses that are listed for sale won't sell? That's because what the industry was missing was someone like me who's not afraid to think outside of the box, employ precise strategy that fits the deal, and use the skill sets and talents that I have to get deals to the Closing Table. I have successfully closed what some of my associates would consider to be an impossible deal, simply because it did not fit into a square box of ideal circumstances. Now, were those deals incredibly difficult? Yes. And I want to help you and your business avoid becoming the impossible deal.

Again, selling a business the right way is an incredibly complex and involved process. It's like brain surgery. If you needed brain surgery you would seek out the top brain surgeon in the book. You want to flip your b z and cash out big? You need to hire the best business broker in the book. That's me. And now I'm in a position to help sellers and buyers alike achieve their goals and put them both on the path to a smooth transition in business ownership.

YOUR NEXT MOVE

So, to answer your question, your next move is to call The Main Man at **1-800-THEMAINMAN** or go to www.flipyourbiz.com and let's get started on your valuation right now. **But, before you call me, do me a favor and flip to page 126**. These are bona fide, unedited testimonials from just a few of the sellers and buyers that I've worked with over the years. What you're reading is pure emotion and gratitude for the services that me and my team have provided to help them realize their dreams.

So now is the time to take the first step. Before you go any further with attempting to sell your business, you need to know how much your business is worth. And if we identify some holes, my chief objective is to help you fix or change your circumstances so that your business becomes flipable for the most cash possible. If your business is in the graveyard, it's not too late to maneuver it into recovery. If your business is above ground and you're ready to sell, I can find ways to help you maximize the value so you can cash out EVEN BIGGER.

My #1 goal is to add YOUR TESTIMONIAL to the rest. So, let's get after it and let's get startec today! Let's **FLIP YOUR BIZ AND CASH OUT BIG!**

APPENDICES

EXIT STRATEGY PLANNING

As we've discussed, your exit strategy is crucial. This is your end game and the way you will map the future of the business and your overall livelihood to win on all levels. So, it has to be intuitive and it has to predict the future. Not only that, you have to start planning your strategy at the right time in order for it to be effective and work for you, your family and your employees. And it might feel counter-intuitive or just plain wrong to start planning for the end while you're still dominating the game and the business is on top. But that's why you got into business in the first place; to win and to dominate. The exit strategy ensures that you will continue to win after the game is over.

In chapter two we discussed when is the right time to start planning your exit strategy and we said that, traditionally, you should start thinking about it when your business reaches Phase 4 of the business lifecycle when you're sustaining. What I told you is that in real-world, the real-talk phase when you should start planning is when you reach **Phase Point of No Return** – when you are absolutely certain that you can't see yourself owning and operating your business anymore and it could be for any number of reasons. My goal is to help you plan your exit strategy before decline and decay sets in so that you can flip, cash out big and not have to suffer the after effects of **The Inevitable Wrong** (selling for the wrong reasons, at the wrong time, to the wrong buyer, at the wrong price).

First, here are the different types of exit strategies or succession plans to consider and you need to determine what options are foreseeable and plausible for you:

1 Keep the business in the family

2 Sell the business to key management or employees

3 Sell the business to another business within the same industry (competitor)

4 Sell on the open market to new buyers

5 Let it die and try to liquidate

And that decision is based on your answers to these real-talk questions that you must ask yourself:

1 Where do I realistically see the business in 5-10 years?

2 What will be my role be as the business changes and evolves? Can this business survive without me? Do I want to grow or do I want to go?

3 What is my business worth today and what am I doing to maximize the value in the future?

4 Is succession probable or even possible? If so, who is the likely successor (family, key staff, new buyer?)

5 If there is no probable, possible succession plan...then what?

6 Is there a life for me and my family after this business and what will t look like?

7 What do I want to do with the rest of my life?

The answers to these very key questions might come into clearer focus after doing some due diligence on the current state of the business and putting some action into whatever course correction might be necessary in crucial operational aspects of the business.

EXIT PLANNING ACTION

Here's what we need to do to devise the right strategy for your end game so we can maximize the value of the business before you list.

CLEAN UP THE FINANCIALS

Do an audit of your books over the past 3 years, which means pull your tax returns and learn how to read them. Pay particular attention to **what we discuss in chapter 3**.

BUILD A SOLID MANAGEMENT & SALES TEAM

Your business' value will absolutely plummet if it cannot operate without you. So, you must start staging and implementing an organizational hierarchy based on defined roles and responsibilities of upper level, lower level and special skilled individuals. Get them into their roles and let them start exercising some autonomy so they can build on their areas of expertise within the business. This also includes building a high-octane, kick-ass sales team to continually bring in new prospects and opportunities and to build a never-ending pipeline. Point blank: no sales, no business, no business value.

IMPROVE YOUR SALES & MARKETING STRATEGY

This is key, especially if your business is starting to see some decline in revenues – and even it if hasn't. Again, not only am I a business broker, my core strength as an entrepreneur is in sales and marketing. This is what I do: sales, marketing, branding: the holy trinity to business success and the key to increasing the value of your business. I bring in my reinforcements, evaluate and restructure the sale team as well as build upon the marketing strategy (direct, online, social media, referral business, offers & discounts) so we can tee it up and make it better than what it is now.

DOCUMENT INTERNAL PROCESSES & SYSTEMS

Write an SOP cocument for every process that is performed to operate the business (sales, marketing, operations, fulfillment, customer service, human resources, contingency plans, etc.) so that you have clear and documented standards of procedure. Update it as you evolve and improve upon your systems. This not only boosts efficiency within the business, it makes the business look so legit and new buyers will appreciate the value of it during the transition.

INVENTORY YOUR ASSETS

Do it and update it bi-annually or as needed. It should include all of your physical assets such as furniture, computer and business equipment, specialized equipment, fleet, product, and even office supplies. Don't over-estimate. Don't under-estimate.

CONTRACT CHECK

Pull and review every single contract that you have with customers, suppliers, vendors, employees and make sure that they all have clear Ts & Cs and have been "executed" by all parties involved. If anything looks shotty or looks like it could provide headaches for you down the road because of vague, one-sided language or because they are legally out of compliance, get them re-drawn and re-signed. This is all part of covering your ass. Also, as we discussed in chapter four, you should start thinking about drawing up new employee contracts that contain a **stay** clause or some type of agreement that incentivizes key staff to stay in the business during and after an impending transfer of ownership (sale, succession to family, etc.). A new buyer is going to see the value in keeping key players onboard after he or she takes over the operation.

WATCH YOUR TIMING

Knowing that it could take years to properly plan an exit strategy and prepare your business for sale, you have to use your keen instincts on when is the right time to start preparing. Start off by looking at the things you can do today and put them into action. Don't put it off because your opportunity or necessity to sell might come sooner than you initially plan.

Be prepared. Stay ready so you don't have to get ready.

START YOUR BIZ PROFILE NOW

A comprehensive business or company profile is great to have at your fingertips when you're ready to start preparing the business for sale. It's a snapshot of the company's history, structure and operation, which can be quickly produced when you start engaging with a business broker. Go to www.flipyourbiz.com, download my quick, simple form and then send it to me at info@flipyourbiz.com so we can get the ball rolling.

COMPANY SUMMARY

- Company Name
- Name of the founder(s)
- Legal Structure (S-Corp, C-Corp, LLC, Partnership, Sole Proprietorship)
- Date established
- Corporate officers
- Number of employees; types of employees or independent contractors
- Brief summary of the company history
- Business description
- Website and Social Media

OPERATIONS

- Description of products, services and overall business activities
- Main location & how many years at that location
- Other locations
- Market area or regions serviced (local, state, nationwide, international)
- Building description and lease information
- Key employee/management titles, job descriptions, compensation and benefits packages
- Hours of operation
- Operation equipment and inventory list

FINANCIALS

- Accounting method (accrual or cash basis)
- Three-year summary of annual revenue, net profits and owner(s) discretionary earnings
- Current P&L
- Number of customers and % of annual revenue of each

MARKETING

- Industry information
- Competition

- Competitive advantages
- Market geographical area
- Marketing strategy with examples of each (website, social media, direct marketing, online, telemarketing)
- Growth potential and untapped markets

INSIGHTS

- What are your business strengths?
- What are your business weaknesses?
- Business challenges and strategies on how they can be overcome
- Why are you selling the business?
- What do you think the value of your business is?
- What do think potential buyer concerns will be and your transition plan that can resolve each concern?
- Will you consider seller-financing?

THE SERIOUS BUYERS CHECKLIST

The Serious Buyer will come with their game face on and a playbook that contains their checklist. As we get deeper and deeper into the transaction, more questions will develop on the checklist. We need to be prepared to answer so that your business becomes the right one for them. You can also find this checklist on my website www.flipyourbiz.com.

☑ Is the business broker legitimate and is he willing to take time with me?

☑ Are there options for me to explore?

☑ Is the business I'm inquiring about viable and legitimate for me to explore?

☑ Why is the business I'm inquiring about for sale? What's wrong with it?

☑ Is the seller willing to take the time to meet with me, be transparent and show me the business operation?

☑ How much can I make in this business and will I make what I need to provide me with the lifestyle I want?

☑ How much is the business making now? Can they show me the money?

☑ Is the business earning enough income to sustain the operating costs and provide cash flow? Can I realistically sustain that and even build on it?

☑ Is the business in a secure market or industry?

☑ Can I expand it? Are there growth opportunities?

☑ How easy is the business to operate?

☑ Will key staff stick around after I take over?

☑ Do I like the business? Do I like the location?

☑ Can I see myself dedicating the majority of my time to making this business successful?

☑ Is the price negotiable?

☑ Can I use inefficiencies in the operation as leverage at the negotiating table? Can I correct the inefficiencies?

☑ Is the business financeable and will the seller extend seller financing?

☑ How invested is the seller and the broker into making sure I succeed in the business? Will they be available to me after the closing?

☑ How smooth will the transition be? Will I lose customers or staff?

☑ Can I flip the business in the future?

FREE VALUATION WORTH $2500

FLIP YOUR BIZ TESTIMONIALS

Still not convinced that The Main Man is the best in the business to flip your biz and cash you out BIG? Read a few of these real and certifiable testimonials that I've received over the years from both business buyers and sellers. No one transaction was the same but we all made it to the closing table and scored that **Three-Way Win!**

BUYER TESTIMONIALS

Dear Anthony,

I wanted to take a moment to thank you for recommending the Home Health Care business to Bonnie & I. For years we have been looking for the perfect fit with our business and professional background where we could not only serve the public but also make a nice living doing so. I am happy to say that you nailed it perfectly for us.

As you are aware, this transaction from start to finish was difficult and complicated when the Small Business Administration and government regulatory restrictions are involved. You and your team of professionals guided us perfectly through the process and were always available around the clock. Additionally, your dedication to both the buyer and seller has been nothing short of amazing as our transition was seamless! You will be a great part of our future success.

Thank you for a wonderful opportunity and providing us with a bright future. You are "The Main Man."

Respectfully yours,
Matthew Goldberg
President & CEO
Nurse One Home Health, LLC

★

Dear Anthony,

I wanted to take a moment to thank you for helping me find the right company for my family and I which was accomplished with the acquisition of T&D Air Conditioning. You did a fantastic job of communicating, managing the project, and keeping all involved parties on task to ensure no deadlines were missed. It has been a pleasure working with you and hope we can work together again in the future.

As you know, the acquisition was difficult and faced many challenges from the start; however, you and your team helped us get to the finish line. Our biggest obstacle in this acquisition was finding a bank willing to finance the deal because I did not have the necessary Class A Air Conditioning license required to operate the business and needed the seller to qualify my company. You worked diligently to help me find the right bank to finance the acquisition and made sure all parties (myself, the seller, & the bank) were all comfortable. We talked to four different banks before we found the right one. Additionally we ran into some delays with me using an IRA as portion of my equity injection since the Small Business Administration changed the rules midway through the process. During this delay, again, you and your team did a wonderful job at keeping the deal together with myself and the sellers. I really appreciate all your effort and hard work.

You were the instrumental piece to accomplishing this acquisition and providing my family and I with this great opportunity. Thank you. I would highly recommend you and your team for anyone looking to work with a business broker in Florida.

Regards,
Chris Durig
President
CCD Holdings, Inc. DBA T&D Air Conditioning

★

Dear Anthony,

Debi and I would like to thank you for the successful purchase of our new business. You and your staff were on point and stayed on top of the transaction every step of the way and exceeded all our expectations. A great deal of thanks to Donna for preparing all the documents and making sure deadlines were met, and all parties were kept in the loop.

When we first came into your office and explained our past dealings with other brokers and the fact that we had spent money on appraisals and the deal did not close, you assured us and gave us your word that this would not happen in your case. YOU WERE RIGHT !! Also in dealing with the banks that you do business with, it was a pleasure working with them and along with yourself was able to get the job done.

We can say with great certainty that you are our new business broker of choice moving forward and we are looking forward to growing our new business and re-listing it with you and purchasing other business as well in the future. We will also be recommending your services to all our friends and family and anyone who wants to buy or sell a business.

Sincerely, Andy & Debi
Nationwide Medical Transportation Services, INC DBA:
Tri-Country Medical Transportation

★

While sitting in the middle of another dreary March snowstorm in Long Island, I was contemplating the purchase of a few different types of area businesses, when I came upon an internet ad for the "Sale of a building and accounting firm in Sunny and Warm South Florida, within walking distance of beautiful beaches." I must say that while I was intrigued, was hardly sold on the idea at first. But I did put an initial call to Anthony Caliendo. Still, even after our first talk, I was not sold on buying this business, especially since due to family reasons, I had no intention of moving to Florida – thus, if this were to happen – it would be a "long commute."

But Anthony is, I must say, a remarkable businessman and salesman. He does not pressure you, but he is persistent. He does not entrap you, but offers a multitude of suggestions on how the deal can work for both parties. And he is not limited by geographic boundaries – I think he believes that the whole world is in play to make a deal. And he understands that there needs to be a good chemistry between buyer and seller – but yet, is smart in knowing that too much communication in the early stages between the parties may not be so good – especially in my case – over the phone (when you can't read a person's face and could easily be misinterpreted). So communication between buyer and seller was assured of no misunderstandings, as Anthony was in the middle of all negotiations. Anthony took no sides – he was working for both of us. There is a genius in this ability, to know just what to say and when. And when I said to Anthony: "I don't know how I could work this – living in New York and commuting in Florida". Anthony had an answer as well: "You have many options here – you can take it as slow as you want or as quickly as you want. You can hire staff if you can't be down here, but you can make it work with any other number of options; and you can rent out unneeded space or not."

He has the experience and know-how to make things happen. Anthony made this deal happen – No doubt about it. If you want the best broker to be found, then I highly recommend bring Anthony on with his team – you'll be in great hands.

Sandy W. CPA – Pompano Beach & New York.

SELLER TESTIMONIALS

To The Main Man Anthony Caliendo,

We had originally started looking for a broker to sell our business years prior to meeting Anthony. We anticipated our business value to be $800,000 and we were met with low listing prices around $400,000-$500,000 price range. Disappointed, we put the decision to sell on hold until we heard Anthony on the radio and decided to see what The Main Man was all about. After meeting with Anthony and experiencing his expertise in his business, we decided to list with him for more than double what the previous brokers structured ultimately closing at $1,250,000.00 million. Ironically, the evaluation from the third-party evaluation from the bank was $1,255,000.00 which means Anthony was right on the money.

We were presented with multiple buyers and after a very good year in 2019 Anthony raised our listing price another $100,000. After this, we were presented with an excellent buyer who presented us with a full price offer. Anthony was there through the entire process of structuring, licensing, due diligence and finally getting us all to the closing table.

His persistence made this process efficient and constantly progressing us to the finish line.

During the due diligence, Anthony shopped through four different banks before finding the right one to process the SBA loan. He also guided us through the process as the SBA changed their rules part way through the application. Through complications and time related setbacks, Anthony was there to support everyone and keep us on track to the closing table.

Anthony and his staff are helpful and great people to work with and I am very glad we chose The Main Man to sell our business. No one could have gotten us a better price and the experience exceeded our expectations. You are really The Main Man.

Thank you, Anthony,
Dean Diciaula &Theodore Gill
T&D Air Conditioning Inc.

★

To Anthony Caliendo,

We approached Anthony after he successfully sold my brother-in-law's pool remolding and landscape business in Delray Beach, FL in late 2019. Our company was quite different in that it was a Medicare Certified Home Health Agency, in South Florida and we had our reservations, in that Anthony had never sold a home health agency previously. Very quickly he allayed any concerns we had by producing not one, but multiple Buyers for our company in a matter of weeks. With Anthony's guidance, we went under contract with a great couple from New York.

But like any large transaction, the party had only started! The "due diligence" took several months and as expected, there were many times the deal got off track because of the legal and/or financial considerations from both parties. But throughout the process, Anthony always rallied the Buyer and Seller and kept everything moving ahead. While egos flared and both parties were repeatedly tested, the deal was successfully closed in Feb. 2020. In the case of our deal, the Buyer secured an SBA loan to finance the deal. SBA loans require extensive personal and financial documentation from the Buyer and my hats-off to him and his Accountant, since they managed to get everything the SBA needed and never held up the deal!

In closing, I can truly tell you that without the skill, dedication and perseverance of Anthony, along with 100's of calls to him made by me and probably the buyer too, this deal would have never closed. And while no Seller ever wants to pay a commission, especially the kind of commissions large deals generate, I can assure you, it was worth every penny! Thanks Anthony to you and your staff at FNBC.

Respectfully,
Bruce & Patty Catanzaro
Nurse One Home Health, LLC

★

Dear Anthony:

I would like to thank you and your competent staff for the outstanding job in the sale of my business. I am extremely pleased with the efficient way it was all handled and with the rewarding outcome.

When I met Anthony, I immediately knew he was the right Broker to sell my business. He offered so many useful recommendations, had an aggressive marketing plan and fresh ideas, that were key in achieving a successful sale.

Anthony was always professional, courteous, knowledgeable, persistent, determined and kept me well informed during the entire process

I can honestly say my experience was smooth, he was always well prepared and on top of things at all times. I now consider Anthony as a friend, one that I continue to communicate with.

I highly recommend him, his services and entire staff to anyone interested in selling or buying a business.

Sincerely,
Juan M. Alfonso
Former Owner
Supreme Seat Covers

Dear Anthony:

I wanted to thank you for the assistance you provided during the sale of our business. It was a pleasure to have met you There was an instant connection from the moment we met. You were very professional from the first day we met while still offering a degree of comfort in the ease of your personality. You have all of the qualities needed to get the job done. I can tell you take your job seriously but also important, you love what you do and it shows in all aspects of your business.

I appreciated the constant contact you and your staff kept with us throughout every phase of the process. While I was afraid of legal complications you assured us that it would all be a smooth transaction with the help of all those resources you bring together to get it all done and finalized. Working with the attorney you recommended was also as smooth and easy as you said it would be. You showed an incredible degree of patience in dealing with the demands of multiple potential buyers and your constant perseverance and unfolding efforts is what made things happen.

There is no doubt in my mind that you are "The Main Man"! I will certainly think of you if ever in the market to buy or sell again and will always recommend you to anyone that may be in need of your services. I wish you the best now and always.

Again, Thank You!

Best Regards,
Carmen Alfonso
Former VP
Seat Savers by Supreme d/b/a Supreme Seat Covers

★

Dear Anthony –

We would like to Thank You, sincerely, for helping us achieve our lifetime goal in selling our businesses. We also would like to thank Donna too for her expertise and assistance in getting our paperwork detailed correctly.

From the first time of Hardy hearing your ad on W10D 610 Sports Talk Radio with Jeff DeForrest and your question "Are you tired of being tired?" ... he felt you would be our "Main Man" broker. I had some doubts about a "guy on the radio" being our liason between 40 years of dedicated work and a simpler lifestyle. After one meeting with you, and presenting our company to you we saw a "light at the end of the tunnel" – and we knew we had found the right man in THE MAIN MAN for the task.

We very much appreciate your care and concern for our business regarding finding the correct buyer to enhance & carry on our business heritage and longevity in the construction field.

Everything in life happens for a reason … who knew that by Hardy listening to DeFo's show, that we would be lucky enough to have you represent us & our businesses, successfully broker & close the deal and allow us to start planning our future.

Thank you, Anthony, you are "The Main Man"! This has been a life changing experience!

Barbara and Hardy
Former Owners
Doetch's Glass & Aluminum CO., LLC

★

Dear Anthony, I would like to thank you and the whole FNBC staff for the successful sale of our business. Your knowledge, diligence, persistence and hard work made the whole process easier than I had expected.

I first heard your advertisement on the Jeff Deforrest morning radio show and asked Jeff about your sales ability. You came highly recommended so I decided to give you a call. I was a little hesitant, thinking I would not be able to sell my business for what I thought it was worth. After 1 week when I had an offer for the evaluation made me a believer in your expertise as a broker.

From the beginning of the due diligence process, to working with the bank, pre-qualifying the buyers, providing necessary documents, keeping me update, to closing, you were on top of it pushing everything along.

My special thanks to Donna who providing me with any information request in a prompt professional manner.

I will be recommending your services to all of my family, friends and business associates who are interested in selling their business.

Thanks again.

Sincerely,
Olivia Katrych
Former Owner
Tri County Medical Transportation Inc

★

I first heard about Anthony Caliendo while listening to the Dan Lebatard show, his advertisement impressed me as an aggressive marketer of businesses. So when I decided to sell my business I needed someone that would be aggressive and innovative in his marketing campaign. After our first meeting I knew I retained the right man for the job because his marketing plans included advertising to prospects out of the State of Florida that wanted to come to Florida to own an Accounting Practice.

Well his marketing campaign was immediately successful because both interested parties were from out of state, which led to an offer and quick closing. I would recommend Anthony to Anyone who is serious in selling their business quickly and efficiently.

Sincerely,
Michael Kerlew
Former owner
EZ Accounting & Tax Service.

HIRE THE SALES ASSASSIN TODAY

THE SALES ASSASSIN BOOK TRILOGY

DON'T HIRE A REALTOR. HIRE A CLOSER.

ABOUT THE AUTHOR

"The business world changes around us with relentless speed and intensity. It takes great vision to not only see these changes, but to also anticipate and react with the tenacity to sustain success."

Few business leaders possess the innate skills to maneuver the modern-day challenges of today's business. Anthony Caliendo is one of these self-made men, an entrepreneur and corporate visionary. To thrive in business and beyond, Anthony learned to project and understand the trends and dynamic forces that shape business and to always move swiftly and strategically.

Anthony is a professional salesman, marketing machine, and sales leadership coach with supersensory sales skills, proven success in sales strategy and corporate leadership, and has generated hundreds of millions in sales revenues; he trained thousands of sales pros in various industries over 25 years to define him as the Ultimate Sales Assassin Master! Today he is a motivational sales speaker and author of the international best-selling, multi-award-winning book, The Sales Assassin: Master Your Black Belt in Sales. He was also a featured Thought Leader® and co-author of the book Cracking the Code to Success with Brian Tracy and The Recipe for Success with Jack Canfield.

Anthony discovered his entrepreneurial instincts early in life. At 18, he became the youngest manager at that time to oversee Chicago Health Clubs and built the World Gyms with Arnold Schwarzenegger. Afterwards, Caliendo went on Wall Street as a stock broker where his instincts and thirst for sales domination accelerated. Achieving financial success on Wall Street and other business ventures, Anthony mastered the art of branding when he became known as "The Main Man" in the mortgage business, architect of one of South Florida's most successful mortgage and real estate companies and an on-air celebrity.

In 2008, during one of the worst economic downturns, Anthony reinvented himself and became the #1 Italian Cheese Salesman in the USA known as the "The Big Cheese" at 1-800-

BIGCHEESE, directing his manufacturer's national and global expansion.

Anthony continues to keeps his sales and entrepreneurial skills sharp and in full practice. In 2017, he revived "The Main Man" and 1-800-THEMAINMAN, and is one of South Florida's premier business brokers and residential real estate brokers, successfully listing and selling millions in businesses and homes for sale.

His outrageous and relentless mentality drove Anthony to construct a fail-proof sales model encompassing specific skillsets and concepts that became the foundation of sales training. The motivational themes of his sales experience inspired him to write The Sales Assassin and become a sales motivational speaker and sales coach to salespeople in all industries.

Anthony has showcased his sales strategies on radio and on CBS, NBC, ABC and FOX and a contributing writer in industry mags including Salesforce, Small Biz Daily, The Canadian Business Journal, Focus Magazine, TK Business Magazine, AMA Playbook, In Business Magazine and Digital Journal.

Anthony lives and works in South Florida with his wife, Lynette and their eight children.

ROMAN BASI
CONTRIBUTING WRITER

Roman Basi, raised in Southern Illinois, began his working career at a young age umpiring little league base-ball games. He spent his teenage and college years working for his father's varied business interests. These experiences helped develop his future interest in helping small business owners fulfill their business and succession plans.

He graduated from Millikin University obtaining a Bachelor's of Science Degree with a minor in Psychology. After receiving his degree, he continued his studies earning an MBA from Southern Illinois University with an emphasis in Accounting. He continued on to law school receiving his JD (law degree) from Southern Illinois University. He is a licensed attorney in

Illinois, Missouri, Florida and Arizona. Roman is also admitted to the United States District Court for the Southern District of Illinois, the United States Court of Appeals for the 7th Circuit, and admitted to practice in the United States Supreme Court.

Roman is also a licensed Certified Public Accountant (CPA). Roman is also a licensed Managing Real Estate Broker in Illinois with Heartland Realty & Rentals, Inc., a licensed Real Estate Sales Associate in Florida, a licensed Title Insurance Agent with ATG Fund, Inc. and a licensed Private Pilot with an Instrument Rating.

Over the past several years, Roman has worked on many business transactions and has lectured to various regional and national audiences throughout the country, including extensive work in the continuing education field for Attorneys and CPA's as well as providing the education necessary for the Voluntary Tax Return Preparer Registry with the IRS. From these venues he has personally met and worked with business owners through-out the United States. He is President of The Center for Financial, Legal & Tax Planning, Inc. (DBA Basi, Basi & Associates) and is in high demand by business owners for his expertise in financial, legal and tax matters.

Roman has been published in the following publications: The Illinois State Bar Association Section on Federal Taxation, Productivity, Agency Sales, Industrial Distribution, Supply House Times, Distributor Link and the I.D.A. Management Journal.

Roman enjoys working with his father and with their national clientele. He is responsible for many of the legal contracts produced by The Center for Financial, Legal & Tax Planning, Inc. His areas of expertise include mergers and acquisitions, contracts, real estate law, tax and estate planning. Roman is very active in his local community and is a member of numerous associations, and Boards of Directors and has served on various committees. He currently serves on the International Business Brokers Association Education Committee. He participates in the Illinois Department of Transportation Adopt-A-Highway Program. Roman is also a current member of the Arizona, Florida, Illinois and Missouri Bar Associations, the American Institute of CPA's (AICPA) as well as a past member of the National, Illinois, Florida, Sarasota and Egyptian Boards of Realtors. He has previously served as a member on the Illinois State Bar Association's Federal Taxation Section Council Committee, Director for the Illinois Association of Realtors,

Officer and two term President for the Egyptian Board of Realtors, Director for the Marion, Illinois Chamber of Commerce, and volunteer for the Women's Center of Carbondale, Illinois.

Roman and Brandi, his wife of 21 years, have two children: Marissa (19) and Alexis (16). They reside in Marion, Illinois. He enjoys spending time with his wife, attending his daughters' various activities, playing golf, flying a 1982 Piper Saratoga and is an avid St. Louis Cardinals' and Tennessee Titans fan.

www.ingramcontent.com/pod-product-compliance
Lightning Source LLC
Chambersburg PA
CBHW072351200326
41519CB00015B/3730